Hedgerow History

Ecology, History and Landscape Character

Gerry Barnes and Tom Williamson

WIND*gather*
PRESS

Published by: Windgather Press Ltd, 29 Bishop Road, Bollington,
Macclesfield, Cheshire SK10 5NX

Distributed by: Central Books Ltd, 99 Wallis Road, London E9 5LN

British Library Cataloguing-in-Publication Data
A catalogue record for this book is available from the British Library

ISBN 1–905119–04–6

Designed, typeset and originated by Carnegie Publishing Ltd,
Chatsworth Road, Lancaster

Printed and bound by CPI Bath Press

Contents

List of Figures

Abbreviations

CRO	Cambridgeshire Records Office
LRO	Lincolnshire Records Office
NRO	Norfolk Records Office
PRO: TNA	Public Record Office: The National Archives
WSRO	West Suffolk Records Office

Acknowledgements

A great many people have helped with the research presented in this volume. Surveys of hedges in numerous individual Norfolk parishes were carried out by: P. Adams, Steve Bird, Mary Brewster, Brena Bowler, Julie Champeney, P. Chapman, J. Christmas, C. Collins, M. Collins, J. H. Dawson, Heather English, R. A. Flatt, F. Godwin, N. W. B. Green, W. Green, Ruth Hadman, Carol Haines, R. Harrison, E. Hoyos, Peter Hickling, Kay Ingleton, Willis Johnson, D. Jones, Peter and Anne Kay, Pauline Keeler, M. Killen, Philip Lazaretti, B. M. and G. F. Leake, N. K. Lee, Keith Lovett, R. W. Maidstone, Anne Martin, G. H. Martin, John Mott, R. W. Newstead, B. Nixon, D. Page, L. and A. Porter, M. Rivett, E. Robins, Ann Russell, Kate Skipper, Evelyn Smith, P. Thimbleby, Heidi Thompson, Audrey Valentine, Tony Van Poortvliet, R. and J. A. Welch, G. A. Wallace-Talvitie, Nicola Whyte, Paul Wilkin, and June Wright. In addition, students on the Landscape History course at the University of East Anglia recorded hedges in Wymondham and Kirstead, while Clare Hickman surveyed numerous examples in the Cawston area as part of her MA dissertation. But our greatest debt is to Lucy Whittle, Anne Wood and Patsy Dallas, who undertook a large number of targeted and meticulous surveys, and also offered numerous very useful suggestions and observations. We would like to thank all these individuals, and also all the many landowners who welcomed them on to their land.

Many of the photographs were supplied by Graeme Cresswell; Gary Battell supplied Figure 18. The others are by the authors, although Figure 4 would not have been possible without Eric de Saumarez's aeroplane. Phillip Judge and David Fox prepared the drawings, graphs and maps.

Many other people have also offered help, advice or information, and we would like to thank in particular Jo Parmenter, Richard MacMullen, Graham King, A. Hassell Smith, Jon Gregory, and Sarah Harrison. The awesome task of inputting over 2,800 entries into the computer database was carried out by Sarah Spooner. Lastly, we would like to thank the John Jarrold Trust, who provided generous financial support for this project.

CHAPTER ONE

Hedges and Enclosure

Introduction

This book is about hedges – about their origins and development over time, and the marked variations they exhibit in species content and diversity. It concentrates on the hedges of a single English county – Norfolk – but it is not simply about this one region. Instead, it uses Norfolk as a case study, from which more general lessons about the history of hedges can be learnt. No apologies are offered for devoting a book solely to the subject of hedges, for they play a crucial role in the rural landscape. They are the most common form of field boundary in Britain: even in highland areas they were usually the preferred form of enclosure on the lower, more sheltered ground. They have a central place in English culture, have given their name to numerous plants and animal species, and have been incorporated into many phrases and expressions: we talk of hedgehogs and hedge sparrows, of particular issues being 'hedged about with doubt', or of people 'hedging their bets'. Above all, hedges are vital to wildlife conservation, for in a countryside which is, for the most part, intensively farmed, hedges provide one of the places where a wide variety of plant and animal species are able to survive, and also form corridors along which they can move, and colonise new locations.

We usually think of a hedge as a line of shrubs which is, or was once, managed in such a way as to provide a stock-proof barrier. But even today we sometimes use the term in a rather wider sense. The great banks of earth and stone which enclose the fields in parts of Cornwall and Devon are 'hedges', in spite of the fact that many have only a rather meagre covering of shrubs. In the past, definitions were more blurred. The Old English word *gehægan*, hedge, originally meant any form of enclosure or fence, and both medieval and post-medieval documents sporadically refer to 'dead hedges' – that is, lines of brushwood staked to form a barrier. As late as 1815 such hedges were said to be widely used in Dorset, Kent and elsewhere (Boys 1813, 61; Stevenson 1815a, 172) Some memory of this form of boundary is still perpetuated in the ceremony of the 'Penny Hedge', or penance hedge, which takes place each year at Whitby in Yorkshire. In 1159 three knights, while hunting in Eskdale, pursued a wild boar into a hermitage: the hermit tried to save the animal but they attacked and mortally wounded him. The Abbot of Whitby ordered that they should serve an unusual penance: they and their descendants should forever, on the Eve of the Ascension, erect a 'hedge' of stakes and branches on the foreshore at Whitby, sturdy enough to withstand the incoming tide. Even the conventional, modern definition of a 'hedge' may be problematic. While in most districts of England a hedge is a well-defined, relatively narrow affair, in some areas wider and more sprawling strips of vegetation divide the fields, blurring the line between a hedge and a linear wood. The 'shaws' of the Kentish Weald are an extreme example, but in any area a period of neglect can convert a hedge into a long, narrow copse. In this short volume we will, however, be concerned almost exclusively with hedges as usually defined – lines of shrubs which form field boundaries.

The form and management of hedges

Hedges might be valued today primarily for their scenic qualities, and for their role as wildlife habitats, but all originally had a practical purpose in the farming economy. In the period before the development of barbed wire they were the main method, at least in the lowlands, of providing a stock-proof barrier. But to do this they had to be regularly managed, for a line of shrubs left to its own devices will soon become tall and 'leggy', allowing gaps to form through which livestock will inevitably find their way. Traditionally, the most common method of management was by *laying* or *plashing*, normally carried out during the winter, a relatively slack time of the farming year (Muir and Muir 1997, 96–104; Brooks 1975) (Figure 1). Laying involves a number of distinct procedures. The hedge is first hacked back rigorously with a billhook and any lateral suckers removed. So too is dead material and any unwanted species – those which might harbour pests (such as barberry) or which provide a poor barrier to stock (such as elder). Next, the principal stems are cut roughly three-quarters of the way through, at an angle of between 45 and 60 degrees and at a height of between five and ten centimetres above ground level: they are then bent downwards at an angle of 60 degrees or more so that each 'pleacher' (as the principal stems are usually called) overlaps its neighbour. In the spring, when growth resumes, a thick, impenetrable wall of vegetation is created. There was once a large number of local and regional forms of laying but today the main distinction is between Midland practice on the one hand, and Welsh and south-western practice on the other. In the Midlands the hedge is first cut back with particular thoroughness and the 'pleachers' are then bent over and woven around vertical poles of ash or hazel, called 'stabbers', spaced along the hedge at intervals of about two-thirds of a metre. The bushy or 'brush' side of the hedge is laid away from the associated ditch, to afford some protection from livestock. Long rods of elm or hazel, called 'hethers' or 'binders', are used to keep the stakes and the 'pleachers' in place, forming a kind of continuous 'cable' along the top of the hedge. Many local and regional variations in Midland practice are recorded by early agricultural writers. In Bedfordshire, for example, it was usual to lay each side of the hedge in turn, after a gap of several years, to ensure that it remained stock-proof; while in

FIGURE I.
A recently 'plashed' or
'laid' hedge at the
National Hedge Laying
Championships at
Fakenham in Norfolk.

Northamptonshire and Leicester the hedges were laid in such a way that they grew particularly tall and thick – the so-called 'bullfinches', or bull fences, designed to contain the beef cattle which were a particular speciality of the region (Brooks 1975).

In the Welsh method, which is also found across much of western England, the hedge is less drastically cut back prior to laying, and the 'brush' or twiggy growth remaining after thinning is often laid so that it projects on both sides of the hedge alternately – that is, the hedge is 'double brushed'. 'Crooks', crook-shaped stakes, are often used to hold down the pleachers, and brush-wood is frequently added to the base of the hedge to provide an additional barrier and to protect the new growth. As a consequence, hedges in these areas were traditionally denser, and often wider, than those in the Midlands, perhaps because sheep were more important than cattle in their economies: sheep are much better than cattle at scrambling through gaps at the base of a hedge.

Archaeological evidence suggests that laying was already practised in pre-history. By the time that the first agricultural texts and treatise made their appearance, in the sixteenth century, it seems to have been regarded as the usual method of hedge management. John Fitzherbert's *Booke of Husbandrie*, for example, which was published in 1523, included a chapter on 'How to plashe or pletche a hedge'. This gave instructions on how to lay a newly-planted

3

hedge, after twelve years' growth; how to lay a long-established hedge; and how to deal with outgrown hedges, comprising 'great stubbs or trees, and thinne in the bottome that Cattell may go under or betweene the trees' (Fitzherbert 1534, 23). But plashing was never, in fact, the only method of management. In some districts hedges were regularly *coppiced*. Coppicing is a term usually employed to describe the traditional management of woods, in which most of the trees and shrubs were cut back to a stump or *stool* every ten to fifteen years. Rapid regrowth ensured a ready supply of straight 'poles', suitable for firewood, fencing, building materials and a range of domestic uses. Hedges could be managed in a similar way. Their constituent shrubs could simply be cut down, at intervals of between ten and twenty years: usually to within a few centimetres of the ground but sometimes (in East Anglia especially) at a height of around 0.6–1 m (Kent 1796, 182; Stevenson 1815b, 212). This method required less skill than laying, but more careful farm management, for the new growth needed to be protected from browsing livestock for several years. Where (as was often the case) substantial ditches accompanied the hedge, animals were simply excluded from the unditched side for the necessary period. Alternatively, or in addition, the hedge might be temporarily protected with hurdles or lines of staked brushwood.

We know little about the geographical distribution of coppicing and laying in the period before the late eighteenth century, and it probably changed significantly over time: by then, it was complex and evidently the outcome of a range of factors. Not surprisingly, coppicing was usual in certain primarily arable districts, such as East Anglia. Because fewer animals were kept on farms, it was easier to protect the new growth of a coppiced hedge from browsing. Yet coppicing was also widely practised in some livestock-farming areas, such as Lancashire (Stevens 1815b, 212). Coppicing produced rather more wood than laying, and in early times hedges were often valued for the fuel they produced as much as for the barriers to livestock that they provided, so population density, and the size of the local demand for firewood, may also have been factors in deciding which method of management predominated. The situation is further complicated, however, by the fact that the two practices were not entirely mutually exclusive: hedges might normally be coppiced, but plashed or laid when they began to grow gappy. Moreover, some local traditions recorded in the early nineteenth century combined elements of both practices. Thus in Middlesex, it was usual to cut down a hedge every ten or so years 'to within a few inches of the bank'; a 'very thin hedge' was then formed from a few remaining stems, supplemented by stakes. Within two or three years the vegetation had recovered enough to provide a reasonably stock-proof barrier (Middleton 1813, 150).

When hedges were laid or coppiced any associated ditch was usually scoured out. Together with the bank on which the hedge grew, ditches helped provide a secure barrier against livestock but, more importantly on heavy land, they helped drain the adjacent fields and were connected – via a complex maze of similar drains – to natural watercourses. The soil dug out of the ditch was usually dumped on the adjacent hedge bank: this explains the traditional legal position regarding the line of rural property boundaries, which are deemed to run not along the line of the hedge itself, but along the further side of the ditch. The ditch, that is, is considered to be part of the property on the *other* side of the hedge.

Hedges have a number of other important characteristics. Most farmland trees were grouped within them, rather than being scattered across the fields, where they might get in the way of ploughs and carts. Some were managed as *standards*, and left to grow naturally for 80–100 years, when they would be felled and used for timber. But in most districts, at least before the start of the nineteenth century, the majority were *pollarded* – that is, managed as aerial coppices, cut at intervals of 10–15 years at a height of 2–3 m above the ground (Rackham 1986, 65–7). Oak was the most common hedgerow tree but ash and elm were also frequent; sycamore was important in many northern and western districts, and hornbeam and even maple might on occasion be permitted to grow into mature trees.

Some pollards were probably used to produce fodder for livestock, and some trees were 'shred' – systematically stripped of their branches, in order to produce a mass of young, succulent side growth which could be stored into the winter. 'Leafy hay' was an important part of peasant economies across much of Europe in earlier times (Halstead 1996; Slotte 2001). Elm and holly were particularly favoured as feed but other species, including oak, will also be happily consumed by livestock (Spray 1981) and it is possible that in some districts hedges themselves were used as a source of fodder, and cut for the purpose in the late summer. Hedges might also have provided some marginal sustenance for humans, in the form of fruit and nuts. Even today the early autumn sees an influx of town-dwellers into the countryside, eager to garner the rich harvest of blackberries.

Partly perhaps because many hedges were originally planted with a range of plants suitable for such a variety of uses, a large number of different species can today be found growing within them. Some of these, if left to their own devices, will develop into sizeable trees: alder, ash, beech, cherry, crab apple, the various kinds of elm, hawthorn, hornbeam, holly, oak, maple, poplar (black, white or aspen), rowan, sallow, sycamore, whitebeam, and goat willow. Others, in contrast, will remain, even if left unmanaged, as relatively low-growing shrubs, such as blackthorn, buckthorn, bullace, dogwood, elder, hazel, guelder rose, privet, wayfaring tree, and the various kinds of rose – dog rose, burnet, field rose and sweet briar. Most of our common hedge shrubs are natives, but some exotic introductions can also be found. Horse chestnut is thus sporadically encountered; lilac is a familiar feature of hedges on some sandy soils; fuchsia is found in parts of the south-west. But, as we shall see, the species found in hedges today are only in part those with which they were originally planted. Many, and in some hedges most, species are adventitious – natural colonists. Indeed, many hedges were originally planted with a single species, usually hawthorn, also known as 'may' or 'whitethorn'. Its common

FIGURE 2.
This species-poor
hedge, largely
composed of hawthorn,
was planted when the
open fields of
Littlebury in north-
west Essex were
enclosed in 1816.

name – from the Old English *gehægen*, hedge – attests its ancient importance in this role. Hawthorn grows quickly, flourishes on almost all soils, and is equipped with particularly unpleasant thorns. Blackthorn, or sloe, has always been the second most popular choice of hedging plant. It has similar advantages to hawthorn but is a strongly suckering species, and thus tends to spread into the adjacent fields, gradually forming a wide linear thicket, unless rigorously managed.

The particular mixture of shrub species found today in hedges displays considerable variation. Many are dominated by hawthorn or blackthorn, with other shrubs relatively limited in numbers (Figure 2). At the other extreme we find hedges which are much more mixed and in which no species is dominant, other than for a few metres of length (Figure 3). Some of these variations reflect local environmental conditions, but some seem to relate to the origins and antiquity of the hedge, and it is this subject which forms our main concern in this book. Why do hedges display these variations? To what extent can they be used to elucidate the origins of particular hedges, and thus the history of the wider landscape? And precisely how, over time, does the flora of a hedge develop?

FIGURE 3.
A typical mixed,
species-rich hedge at
Kenninghall in south
Norfolk. There is no
dominant shrub,
although certain species
have monopolised short
lengths of the hedge.

Woodland and Champion

In order to answer these questions we must first provide some broad context: we must consider, in very general terms, how the pattern of field boundaries developed across England over time. Existing hedges can be of any age – from 1,000 years or more, to less than a day old. But the general antiquity of hedges tends, in broad terms, to vary from region to region. In some districts, a high proportion of hedges was already in existence by *c.*1700. In others, the majority were planted after this date. Many landscape historians use the terms 'ancient' and 'planned' countryside, coined by the historical ecologist Oliver Rackham, to articulate this distinction. The latter kind of countryside he characterised as having 'big villages, few ... roads, thin hawthorn hedges, windswept brick farms, and ivied clumps of trees in the corners of fields'. It was a 'predictable landscape of wide views, sweeping sameness, and straight lines' (Rackham 1986, 5). The ancient countryside, in contrast, he described evocatively as 'The land of hamlets, of medieval farms in hollows of the hills, of lonely moats in the clay-lands, of immense mileages of quiet minor roads, hollow-ways, and intricate footpaths; of irregularly shaped groves and thick

hedges colourful with maple, dogwood, and spindle' (Rackham 1976, 17)
(Figure 4). Although, as Rackham emphasised, versions of these ideal types of landscape can be found all over England, they tend to dominate in discrete blocks. 'Planned countryside' is thus concentrated in the Midland areas of England, in a broad band running from Northumberland to the south coast. 'Ancient countryside', in contrast, is principally a feature of the regions lying to the west, and to the south-east of this belt: of the south-east of England and southern East Anglia, and of the West country and the Marcher counties (Figure 5).

The difference between these two kinds of landscape emerged, in the form in which we see it today, in the period after *c.*1650, but it had much older roots. Sixteenth- and seventeenth-century topographers and agricultural writers often posited a distinction between what they called 'woodland' and 'champion' countryside. In the former, most land already lay in fields surrounded by hedges (thus presenting the 'bosky' appearance which gave this kind of countryside its name), and in addition the landscape displayed a number of other characteristics. Settlement was often fairly scattered, with isolated farms and hamlets in addition to – or in some districts instead of – villages. There were also usually numerous areas of managed woodland, and of open common land, in addition to the enclosed fields. The 'champion', in contrast, was open-field country. Here, farmers dwelt together in large villages and their land took the form of numerous small and unhedged strips, each usually less than half an acre in extent, which were mixed together with those of their neighbours and scattered throughout the territory of each village, or *vill.* 'Ancient countryside' is, more or less, equivalent to what early topographers called the 'woodland'. The 'champion' became, after a number of momentous changes, today's 'planned countryside' (Williamson 2003, 1–8).

Champion landscapes came into existence in Saxon times, and they began to disappear in the fifteenth century, to be replaced by landscapes of hedged fields, although in most districts this process really only got under way after *c.*1650. They were associated with highly communal systems of agriculture. Although each farmer harvested the crops produced on his own strips, the inhabitants of the village combined together for particular tasks, notably ploughing, and the day-to-day operation of agriculture was controlled by a village assembly or manorial court. The strips were grouped into bundles called furlongs, each of which lay under a particular crop each year. These in turn were grouped into fields, often two or three in number, one of which lay fallow or uncultivated each year and was grazed by the village livestock. Their dung restored the nutrients which were depleted by repeated cropping.

Historians often write as if there was only one type of 'champion' land-scape, but in reality there were several. While they all had in common the facts that farmers dwelt in nucleated settlements, and farmed their holdings in intermingled strips and to some extent co-operatively, there were many variations in detail. But there was, in particular, a broad distinction between the 'champion' countryside found on the clays of Midland England, and that which typified the light soils of the heaths, wolds and downs: that is, the chalklands of Wessex, the Chilterns and the south Downs, the Yorkshire and Lincolnshire Wolds, the Cotswolds and the sandy soils of eastern England. The clayland Midlands was an intensively arable area by the thirteenth century. Woodland and grazing were normally in short supply or absent altogether, and the arable strips often extended to the very margins of townships. On the light lands, in contrast, large areas of grazing (although not usually woodland) frequently survived, in the form of chalk downs or acid heaths. This was mainly because the thin, easily-leached soils could only be kept in heart by the regular input of particularly large quantities of dung, and this necessitated the maintenance of great flocks of sheep which were systematically folded by night on the arable, and grazed by day both on the fallows, and on these great areas of rough, permanent pasture. In many of these 'sheep-corn' districts, as early writers called them, the arable strips were grouped into two or three great fields. But in some, rather different, more irregular arrangements could be found (Kerridge 1967, 42–5; Williamson 2003, 79–82).

Such subtle differences in the character of champion landscapes are important to the historian but need not concern us any further here. All that matters in the present instance is that these landscapes, while never completely devoid of hedges, usually had few or none outside the immediate vicinity of the village nucleus. Moreover, they had generally lost most or all of their woodland by the early Middle Ages: Domesday Book shows us that most champion regions, and especially those in areas of light soil, were very sparsely wooded (Rackham 1986, 76–7).

If subtle variations between different forms of 'champion' landscape can be ignored for the purposes of this study, the same cannot be said of the differences between various kinds of 'woodland' countryside. It is sometimes suggested that the distinguishing feature of such landscapes was that open fields were limited in area or absent altogether in medieval times, and that – apart from any areas of common grazing – all the farmland lay in walled or hedged fields. While this is certainly true of some areas, such as the London clays of south Hertfordshire and Essex, in most of these districts open fields of a kind were widespread in the early Middle Ages. These differed, however, in a number of important respects from those found in the champion areas. Most were 'irregular' in character, to use the jargon of historical geographers. Individual fields were often smaller and more numerous than in Midland districts and they were associated with the various small hamlets in a township, rather than with a single nucleated village. In many cases, as in the Chiltern Hills, they were mixed up with hedged fields in individual occupancy, and with extensive areas of common grazing and woodland, but elsewhere – as in parts of East Anglia – they could take up most of the land in the village (Roden 1973; Roberts and Wrathmell 2002, 156–7). Either way, the lands of each farm were usually clustered in the area close to the farmstead, instead of being scattered evenly throughout the area of the township

a)

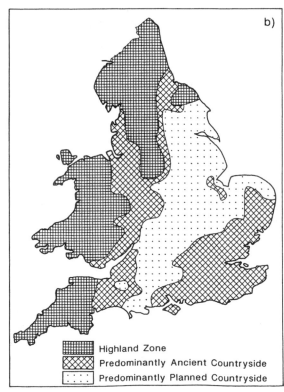

b)

Highland Zone
Predominantly Ancient Countryside
Predominantly Planned Countryside

FIGURE 4.
The ancient countryside
of the south Norfolk
claylands from the air.
Irregularly shaped fields,
sunken lanes and small
patches of woodland are
typical of the landscapes
of early enclosure.

FIGURE 5.
Regions in England.
(a) In the Middle Ages,
Midland areas were
characterised by
extensive, 'regular'
open-field systems
farmed from nucleated
villages: to the south-
east and the west,
settlement was more
dispersed and enclosed
fields, or less 'regular'
forms of open field,
were the norm. This
map shows the areas
which Howard Gray, in
his pioneering book of
1915, considered to have
been characterised by
this 'Midland system'.
(b) Because the
extensive fields of the
'champion' Midlands
were more resistant to
enclosure than those
found elsewhere, this
region remained largely
unhedged until the
eighteenth century. It is
now characterised by
'planned countryside',
with rectilinear fields
and species-poor
hedges. In contrast,
open fields had largely
disappeared from other
regions by c.1700.
These are now areas of
'ancient countryside',
characterised by
irregular fields and
species-rich hedges
(after Rackham, 1986).

or parish. Often, but by no means always, communal controls on the practice of farming were less rigorous and pervasive than in the champion lands. Open fields of this kind were, as we shall see, more easily enclosed than those in champion areas, and by the seventeenth century most had disappeared, thus hardening the visual contrast between 'woodland' and 'champion' regions: the one characterised by enclosed fields, trees and woods; the other by vast, open spaces.

'Woodland' and 'champion', 'planned' countryside and 'ancient', are useful labels but, it need hardly be said, constitute over-simple abstractions. In reality, some kinds of countryside fell, and fall, uneasily between the two categories. This is particularly true of Norfolk, the area which forms the main focus of the research outlined in this short volume.

The progress of enclosure

To understand the origins and character of hedges it is necessary to discuss, in rather more detail than has been normal in books on this subject, the complex history of enclosure in England, from the Middle Ages to the nineteenth century. There is no general agreement over how much of lowland England was occupied by hedged fields and how much by open fields and commons in medieval times. At a conservative estimate, probably less than a third of the land area lay *in severalty* – that is, in privately-owned parcels, free from communal controls – at the beginning of the fourteenth century. By the end of the nineteenth century, in contrast, virtually no open fields, and relatively little common land, remained. They had been removed by the steady progress of *enclosure* – that is, the conversion of land exploited in common, or lying in intermixed parcels and subject to some measure of communal management, to land occupied and managed by private individuals. The spread of privately owned land was intimately associated with the proliferation of hedges and walls, although enclosure in the legal sense was not invariably accompanied by physical enclosure.

Enclosure was achieved in a bewildering number of ways: people often use the word rather loosely, to mean the enclosures carried out by parliamentary acts in the course of the eighteenth and nineteenth century but, as already intimated, these only finished off a process which had been going on for centuries. Historians and geographers have long been interested in this subject and many make a useful distinction between *piecemeal* and *general* enclosure (Yelling 1977, 11–29). Piecemeal enclosure was a gradual process involving a series of private agreements – sales and exchanges – which led to the amalgamation, and subsequent walling or hedging, of groups of contiguous open-field strips. General enclosure, in contrast, was a process involving the whole community of proprietors acting in concert. Lawyers and surveyors ascertained the extent of the property and rights held by each proprietor and then re-organised the landscape at a stroke, usually enclosing the totality of the open land in a parish or township. The two forms of enclosure were not mutually

Middlesex, south Essex and south Hertfordshire, the boulder clays of Suffolk and south Norfolk. In the Midland counties, in contrast, 'regular' open fields were the norm and enclosure, and conversion to pasture, was initially a more complicated and a more traumatic process, often associated with the shrinkage or depopulation of settlements by monopoly landowners. It is in this region that we find the majority of our classic 'deserted medieval villages', cleared to make way for grazing grounds in the fifteenth and sixteenth centuries. But the shift to pasture in the Midlands accelerated from the seventeenth century as the new forms of enclosure by general agreement facilitated the removal of communal agriculture. It continued inexorably in the second half of the eighteenth century, as the new pattern of farming regions developed across England during the 'agricultural revolution' period. Most parliamentary enclosure in the Midlands, which reached a peak in the 1770s, was associated with this process. The vicar of Breedon on the Hill in Leicestershire remarked in 1801 how:

> Within the last 30 years almost all the country north west of Leicester to the extremity of the county has been enclosed ... but on account of a

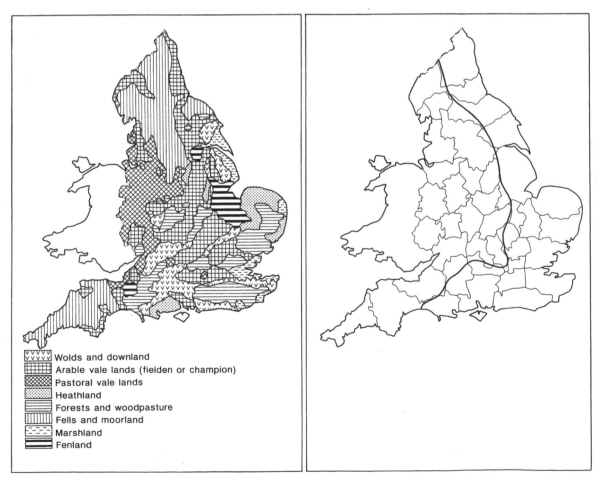

Wolds and downland
Arable vale lands (fielden or champion)
Pastoral vale lands
Heathland
Forests and woodpasture
Fells and moorland
Marshland
Fenland

great proportion of it being converted into pasturage much less food is produced than when it was more generally in tillage (Turner 1982, 53).

On the light-soil champion lands away from the clayland core of the Midlands – in the sheep-corn districts – a continuing emphasis on cereal farming in the early modern period ensured that there was less incentive to enclose. Some townships in the more agriculturally marginal districts were depopulated in late medieval times as their populations drifted away to take up more profitable holdings elsewhere: such places were often laid to sheep-walk or warrens. But for the most part, these remained open landscapes until the eighteenth century, when enclosure began in earnest. This was a time when the new farming systems of the 'agricultural revolution' were being adopted, involving the large-scale cultivation of turnips and clover in regular rotations with cereal crops. These innovations allowed more livestock to be kept and more manure to be produced, and also reduced the need for the great 'nutrient reservoirs' of the heaths and sheepwalks (Williamson 2002, 53–70).

Open-field farming did not in itself preclude the cultivation of the new crops (Havinden 1961), and farmers were capable of altering the basic organisation and layout of their field systems in order to adopt new methods. At Ashley near Scunthorpe in 1784, for example, the landowners and occupiers drew up an agreement 'for Improvement of Lands in the several open Arable fields there by sowing of Turnips and Clover'. Each farmer agreed to fence off some of their strips in the East Field, which were to be 'sown with Turnips or Clover this present year'. The north side of the North Field was to be 'taken in and enclosed the second year of the said term and sown with Clover and Turnips'; while West Field was divided into three parts and farmed according to a four-course rotation. Rights of common grazing were terminated on all the land sown with the new crops, and cottagers with common rights were to be compensated (LRO, Misc Dep 77/16). Other, less drastic arrangements were more common, as at Geddington in Northamptonshire, where it was reported in 1813 that within the fields 'enclosures are made for turnips by temporary fences and clover is also sown' (Pitt 1813a, 76). Nevertheless, there is no doubt that the adoption of the new methods of farming was considerably facilitated by the creation of a landscape of enclosed fields, in which farmers could grow what they wanted, when they wanted. Moreover, the heaths and downs beyond the open fields were often common land, and could only be reclaimed and converted to arable land once they had been enclosed. Enclosure and the adoption of the 'new husbandry' were thus, to a significant extent, connected.

Enclosure on these light soils seems to have increased steadily through the eighteenth century, peaking in a frenzy of parliamentary enclosure during the Napoleonic Wars, a time when grain prices were abnormally high and landowners in a particularly optimistic mood. It was also fuelled by the fact that parliamentary enclosure acts terminated all existing lease agreements – an important consideration, no doubt, in the minds of landowners whose land

FIGURE 8.
Left: in the sixteenth and seventeenth centuries England was a complex mosaic of farming regions. The wolds and downlands, and the heathlands, were arable, 'sheep-corn' areas; other arable countrysides could be found across the Midlands. Elsewhere – in 'forests and wood-pastures', fens, pastoral vales and marshes, and also on the fells and moors of the uplands – the economy was geared more towards the rearing or fattening of livestock (after Thirsk 1987).
Right: by the mid nineteenth century, when James Caird produced his map of English agriculture, this pattern had been transformed. Arable farming was now concentrated in the east of England, as it is today, and pasture farming in the Midlands and west. This great change was one of the key features of the 'agricultural revolution' of the late eighteenth and early nineteenth centuries, and one which had considerable implications for field patterns.

timber supplies, initiated in 1791, included the question: 'Whether the Growth of Oak Timber in Hedge Rows is generally encouraged, or whether the grubbing up of Hedge Rows for the enlarging of fields, and improving Arable Ground, is become common ...?' (Lambert 1977, 708, 724, 748). The answers make it clear that although hedge removal was noted in some western counties (even Devon) it was evidently most marked in the anciently enclosed areas of the south-east and East Anglia, where it was described as 'frequent', 'becoming common', or the 'general practice'. One respondent noted that 'The county of Hertfordshire consists chiefly of Land in Tillage, and by clearing the Hedges of all kinds of Trees they admit of plowing to the utmost Bounds of their Land' (Lambert 1977, 748); while Thomas Preston from Suffolk baldly stated that:

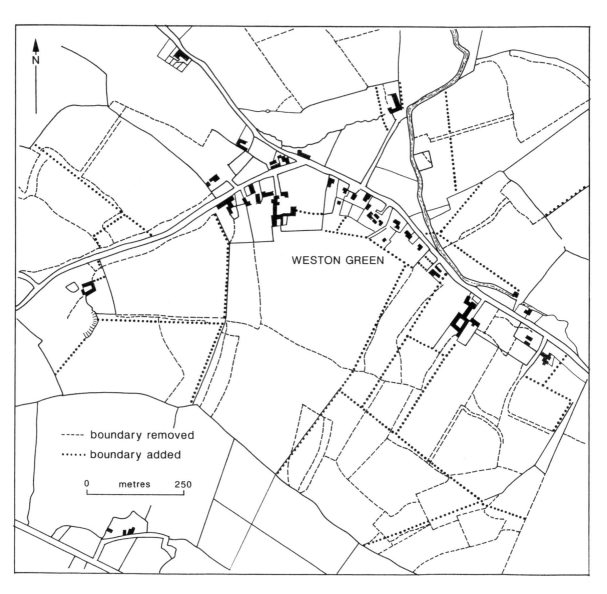

N

WESTON GREEN

----- boundary removed

·········· boundary added

0   metres   250

Underwood, particularly Blackthorn Bushes, in Hedge Rows that spread Two or Three Rods wide, is the true nursery of Oak Timber, but such Rows are a dead Loss and Nuisance in a well cultivated Country. England possessed in the past Age a great Plenty of Oak. Why? Because Cultivation was in a barbarous State. It is the Improvement of the Kingdom ... that has brought about the very good and proper Diminution of Oaks; and it is to be hoped that the Diminution will continue, for if it does not, the Improvement of our Soil will not advance (Lambert 1977, 776).

One observer, writing about the county of Essex in 1801, was able to declare: 'what immense quantities of timber have fallen before the axe and mattock to make way for corn' (Brown 1996, 34). Although landscape historians often use the term 'ancient countryside' to describe the old-enclosed areas outside the Midlands, in some ways this is misleading, for these landscapes continued to develop and change through the eighteenth and nineteenth centuries, and today they include many field boundaries and roads which were only created in relatively recent times (Figure 9).

Recent changes

Farming flourished throughout the early and middle decades of the nineteenth century, buoyed up by population growth and urban expansion. But the late 1870s saw the start of a long agricultural depression. The American railway network reached the prairies of the mid-west, a prime wheat-growing region, allowing European markets to be flooded with cheap grain. From the 1890s, moreover, the development of refrigerated ships allowed cheap meat and dairy produce to be imported on a significant scale from the New World and Australia (Perry 1974, 21–34). The First World War brought some recovery in agricultural fortunes but with the peace came a return to depression which continued, with little real interruption, until the start of the Second World War.

In this new economic climate there were relatively few changes to field boundaries. The area under pasture tended to increase again and there was little money available to make 'improvements' to the farming landscape. Hedges also appear to have been cut and laid less frequently, and often grew tall and wide: a large proportion of saplings was able to develop into mature trees, so that the number of farmland trees in England increased dramatically, from perhaps 23 million in *c.*1870 to around 60 million in 1951 (Rackham 1976, 223). At the same time, barbed wire – invented in America and introduced into Britain in the 1880s – provided an alternative or supplementary way of keeping field boundaries stock-proof, and in many districts traditional forms of management went into decline.

But if the condition of hedges deteriorated in many districts in the first half of the twentieth century, the period after *c.* 1940 saw a more dramatic decline

FIGURE 9.
Weston Colville,
Cambridgeshire. A map
of 1828 in the
Cambridge Records
Office (CRO 124/P83a)
shows alterations to the
field pattern in this
long-enclosed part of
the parish proposed by
the landowner, John
Hall. The majority of
the changes were
carried out: numerous
boundaries were
straightened or
removed. Similar
alterations occurred in
many 'ancient
countryside' areas in
southern and eastern
England during the late
eighteenth and
nineteenth centuries.

in their fortunes. The blockade experienced during the Second World War was followed by an extended period of shortages which lasted into the 1950s. First the national government, and latterly the European Economic Community, introduced a range of subsidies which were aimed at increasing levels of production in order to feed the population. The long agricultural recession was over. Moreover, increased levels of state support were associated with other important changes in the practice and organisation of farming. Farms continued to increase in size, and the widespread adoption of tractors and combine harvesters, and the low cost of artificial fertilisers, ensured that arable farmers no longer had the incentive to keep animals, even horses. Across eastern England especially the numbers of livestock fell drastically, and on many farms hedges were no longer required as stock-proof barriers. And as large machines work most economically in large fields, hedges were increasingly seen as a nuisance, rather than a necessary part of the agricultural environment. They began to be removed wholesale. Bulldozers and mechanical diggers made this a relatively easy task; so too did government subsidies for hedge removal, which began to be paid in 1957 (Figure 10). Between 1946 and 1970 around 4,500 miles (7,245 km) of hedge were destroyed each year in England and Wales, with the greatest losses occurring in the eastern counties (Dowdeswell 1987, 118; Muir and Muir 1997, 225–6). The rate of loss varied considerably from district to district, however. On the whole, areas of ancient countryside, especially in Hertfordshire, Essex, Suffolk and south Norfolk, fared worse than those of more recent enclosure, where the comparatively large, rectilinear field patterns were better adapted to the new modes of farming (Baird and Tarrant 1970). The character of ownership was also a factor, with large landed estates on the whole retaining their hedges with more enthusiasm than small freehold farmers or, in particular, large institutional owners like pension funds.

During the 1970s the rate of destruction in the arable east of England seems to have declined, in part because on many farms there were few hedges left to remove. But mounting opposition from conservationists and the general public, and the resultant withdrawal of government subsidies, also played their part. By 1982 government policy began to change. Under the Farm Capital Grant Scheme subsidies were made available for planting new hedges, and for renovating neglected ones. Nevertheless, destruction continued on some scale, especially in the stock farming areas of the Midlands and the west of England, where hedges were increasingly replaced with wire fences in order to reduce maintenance costs, and where 'paddock grazing' – using sown grass swards and moveable fences – was increasing in popularity. Even where hedges remained their condition, as in the arable east, often deteriorated. Farmers increasingly relied on wire fencing to keep livestock from straying, and the hedges grew tall and 'leggy'.

And it was not only changes in the organisation and practice of agriculture that led to a sharp decline in the fortunes of hedges in the later twentieth century. Many were destroyed by urban and industrial development, or

FIGURE 10.
Barking Tye, Suffolk:
one of the many
thousands of hedges
grubbed out in
England during the
1960s and 70s.

damaged by Dutch elm disease, a particularly virulent strain of which began to affect England in the 1960s. The elm largely disappeared as a tree although it remains common as a shrub (for only when the plant acquires a substantial stem and a well-developed bark does it fall prey to the disease). The outgrown, poorly-managed state of many hedges left them vulnerable to attack, and many grew gappy as a result, or became infested with brambles and elder where large sections of elm had withered and died.

By the 1990s, however, the worst was over. Various government schemes, intended to re-direct resources away from over-production towards nature conservation – especially 'Countryside Stewardship' – gave financial incentives to the replanting of hedges. The grubbing-out of existing hedges was effectively curtailed with the new Hedgerow Regulations of 1997 (later amended in 2002), which finally brought hedge removal within the planning process and laid down a range of criteria on which permission for removal could be denied.

This, in brief, is the long and complex history of hedges in England. We must now turn to the development of individual hedges – to the vexed question of how, over time, their flora develops – which is our main concern in this volume.

CHAPTER TWO

The Hooper Hypothesis

Introduction

It will be apparent from the foregoing account that historians – economic, social, landscape – have long been interested in the process of enclosure and the formation of the fieldscape. Until the 1970s their enquiries were entirely carried out using the evidence of maps and documents but unfortunately, the majority of individual boundaries cannot be dated from such sources. Documents rarely describe the establishment of a particular hedge (or wall) and most parishes in England do not have a surviving map dating from before the eighteenth century. Indeed, for a large number the earliest is the Tithe Award map of the late 1830s or early 1840s. The academic world abhors a vacuum: and into this evidential void came, in the 1970s, an approach which for a while seemed to promise an independent method of dating hedged boundaries.

This approach is today firmly associated with the name of Max Hooper, of the Monk's Wood Experimental Station (later the Institute of Terrestrial Ecology) in Huntingdonshire; but equally important was the contribution made by his colleagues, especially Ernest Pollard. Their joint research came at a time when hedgerows were disappearing at an alarming rate from the countryside, as the process of post-War intensification and rationalisation reached its peak. Not only their own interest in hedges, but also the wide popular interest in their work, can only be understood against this background as, especially, in the arable east of England the familiar, 'traditional' landscape was subjected to an orgy of destruction.

As part of a wider enquiry into the ecology of hedges, Hooper and his colleagues addressed the question of why their shrub content displayed so much variation. They noted that in the area of Huntingdon around the Monks Wood Station the hedges tended either to be dominated by a single species, generally hawthorn or elm, or else were fairly mixed in composition: 'If one found one uncommon shrub in a particular hedge then there would probably be others in there somewhere' (Pollard *et al.* 1974, 76). Moreover, the situation in Huntingdon contrasted with that in other parts of England known to the researchers, such as Kent or Devon, where a much higher proportion of the hedges were of the 'mixed' variety. Hooper and his colleagues examined the possibility that such variations were the consequence of natural factors, such as variations in soil type, and noted how within the

Isle of Purbeck in Dorset the distribution of different types of hedge was strongly correlated with the major geological formations, with mainly black-thorn hedges on the Kimmeridge clays, hawthorn on the chalk, elm on the London clay and mixed hedges on the Purbeck Beds and the Wealden and Bagshot Sands. Yet perplexingly, elsewhere in the country these same forma-tions carried rather different types of hedge: 'For example, on Kimmeridge clay in the Isle of Ely there are hawthorn hedges, on chalk in some areas there are mixed hedges, sometimes very rich as many shrubs such as spindle, wayfaring tree and privet are especially associated with calcareous soils' (Pollard *et al.* 1974, 76). The researchers concluded that the Purbeck correla-tions were not an outcome of natural so much as of historical factors: 'The observed differences must be due to an indirect effect of soil type reflecting different land use histories'.

In this context, they noted the observations made by Grose in his *Flora Of Wiltshire* concerning four hedges in that county: 'two soils, each with an old species-rich hedge and a recent species-poor one. This it seemed could provide the answer, the older the hedge the more species it would have' (Pollard *et al.* 1974, 77). To test this preliminary hypothesis Hooper and his associates set out to examine a total of 227 hedges in the counties of Devon, Lincolnshire, Cambridgeshire, Huntingdonshire and Northamptonshire for which planting dates were available from maps or documents. The hedges were examined using what has since become the standard method: recording in 30 yard sections, and including roses and trees, but excluding climbers like bramble and bryony. The relationship between the hedge's age, and the number of shrub species it contained, appeared to be linear (Figure 11), and regression analysis produced the equation:

Age of hedges = (110 x number of species) + 30 years

In other words, a two-species hedge would be 250 years old, and a five-species one 580 years old. But the equation came with a warning, so often ignored in later studies, that 'the calculation is only very approximate and we could easily be as much as 200 years out *either side*' (Pollard *et al.* 1974, 79; our italics). Further research refined the equation: Hooper calculated that 28 per cent of the observed variation in shrub content could not be explained by age, and acknowledged that soil, climate, and variations in management prac-tices from region to region also played their part. He therefore analysed a more restricted body of data, from a more limited geographical region: 95 hedges, from the clay uplands on the Northamptonshire/Huntingdonshire border. In this more limited sample age accounted for 85 per cent of the variation and the equation was restated as:

Age of hedge = (99 x number of species) − 16

A two-species hedge would now be calculated as being 182 years old, a five-species one 511 years old. Hooper observed that 'The equations calculated so far are all close to one species for every hundred years and this can be used as

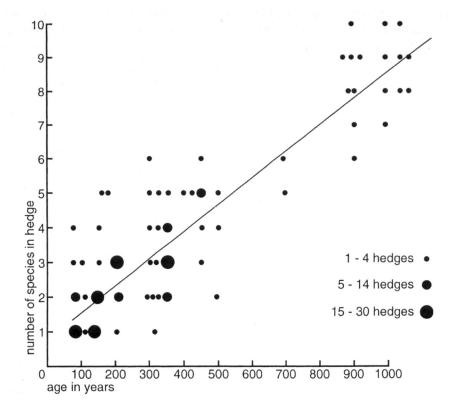

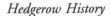

FIGURE II.
The graph produced by
Hooper and Pollard to
show the relationship
between the age of
hedges and the
numbers of species they
contain, based on a
sample of 227 dated
hedges in Devon and
the east Midlands.
From *Hedges*, 1974.

a rule of thumb, provided the large variations are not forgotten' (Pollard *et al.* 1974, 79). It was, of course, in this simplified form that the hedge dating 'method' gained such wide currency in the 1970s and 80s, especially among local historians. Indeed, the first public airing of the theory came, not in the works of Hooper himself, but in W. G. Hoskin's *Fieldwork in Local History*, published in 1967 (Hoskins 1967, 118). Hooper, clearly aware that in such a simple form the approach would have wide appeal, helpfully provided researchers with some advice on surveying methods (Hooper 1970; Hooper 1971; Pollard *et al.* 1974, 80–1). A local calibration should be established if at all possible, using 'at least a dozen' hedges dated by documents. The sample lengths should be selected randomly, and the ends of the boundary should be avoided as these were often atypical of the hedge as a whole, especially where they adjoined an area of woodland. The hedge should be examined from one side only: seedlings should be ignored, but trees included. Given the fact that the method was only able to provide, as he emphasised, a broad indication of the age of a hedge, careful measurement of sample lengths was not warranted: pacing would be quite sufficient.

In his fullest account of the method, published in 1974, Hooper provided a number of brief case studies which showed its potential for historical research, but only when used sensibly, and with due caution. Thus he discussed the parish boundary of Great Gidding in Huntingdonshire, which – on topographic grounds – had evidently been moved at some time in the past in order to include an ancient pond with the suggestive name of Flittermere, 'the disputed pond'. The 'moved' hedge contained twelve species in a thirty yard length, suggesting to Hooper that the change in boundaries had occurred before the Norman Conquest. He concluded: 'This story is, of course, speculative, but the hedge dating technique supplies us with extra information with which to speculate' (Pollard *et al.* 1974, 81–2).

When Hooper and Pollard turned to explaining the observed relationship between age and species content, however, some important complexities and inherent contradictions began to emerge. Many later researchers have tended to ignore the fact that in reality Hooper and his colleagues proposed not one, but two distinct mechanisms which might account for the fact that old hedges are more mixed in their composition than younger ones. The most important of these was colonisation. Most hedges, especially those in former champion areas, were planted with a single shrub – usually hawthorn – and were then colonised, at a relatively standard rate, by new species. Some species colonised fairly rapidly: elder, ash, dog rose, and blackthorn were well represented in both species-poor and species-rich hedges, suggesting 'rapid colonisation and long life of individuals'. Others, however, principally woodland species such as hazel, dogwood, spindle and ('to a lesser extent') maple, were 'poorly represented in species poor hedges but rapidly increase in richer hedges' (Figures 12 and 13). They were slow colonisers, especially hazel, which had failed to colonise one hedge they examined after a period of 150 years, even though it abutted directly on an area of woodland in which the plant was common (Pollard *et al.* 1974, 99–100).

But differences in the time that hedges had been available for colonisation was not the only reason suggested for variations in their species composition. Hooper's colleague Ernest Pollard noted a particular kind of hedge which he termed a 'woodland relic hedge' (Pollard *et al.* 1974, 86–90; Pollard 1973). Such hedges were very mixed and contained large quantities of the slow-colonising woodland species, with 'different shrubs dominant for short lengths, including hazel, dogwood, maple, woodland hawthorn, service and spindle'. In addition, these hedges featured particular herbs in the ground flora growing at their base and in the associated ditch which were – like these shrub species – slow colonisers, closely associated with woodland. The most abundant was dog's mercury (*Mercurialis perennis*), but others, present in smaller quantities, included bluebell (*Hyacinthoides non-scripta*), primrose (*Primula vulgaris*), wood anemone (*Anemone nemorosa*), wood spurge (*Euphorbia amygdaloides*), wood melick (*Melica uniflora*), and yellow archangel (*Lamiastrum galeobdolon*). Pollard and Hooper concluded that these hedges must have originated as assarts in woodland – that is, they had come into existence as fields were cut out of the virgin woodland, as cultivation expanded in early times. Pollard originally argued that 'there was little doubt' that such hedges were 'relics of old woodland, the former wood-edge

vegetation being managed to form a hedge' (Pollard 1973, 351). But in their
1974 book Hooper and Pollard admitted another possibility, that early
colonists had simply improvised hedges around their new plots by gathering
shrubs from the adjacent areas of woodland (Pollard *et al.* 1974, 98).

Many of the hedges containing the largest numbers of woodland shrubs
were, they suggested, of woodland relic type, but not all. Some could be 'very
old single species hedges colonised so thoroughly that the original planting
line had been lost' (Pollard *et al.* 1974, 88). In many such cases, however, the
abundance of woodland species must in itself be an indicator of considerable
age, for such hedges could be found in areas where there is now very little
woodland.

> Their ability to colonise hedges may well depend on the general abundance
> of woodland and so of seed sources in an area. This suggests that when
> woodland was abundant these species colonised hedges much more freely.
> Woodland clearance in East Anglia and the Midlands [the main areas
> discussed by Hooper and Pollard] was well under way by Domesday and
> has continued until, in this century, only a very small proportion of the
> land surface is wooded. This may explain, at least in part, the poor
> representation of these species in recent hedges (Pollard *et al.* 1974, 97).

The implication of this, as Hooper recognised, was that in districts in which
woodland had *continued* to be a prominent feature of the landscape, such as
the Weald of Kent and Sussex, woodland species would not necessarily be
absent from relatively recent hedges in the same way. In such districts 'it could
well be that the relationship with age is different' (the relatively few hedges
which he and his colleagues had examined in this region could not be dated
by documentary means).

The distribution of 'woodland relic hedges', Hooper and Pollard suggested,
might provide additional information about the history of the landscape. In
particular, it could help identify districts in which large quantities of woodland had survived relatively late into the Middle Ages, and in which many
fields had in consequence been reclaimed directly from the 'wastes' rather than
being enclosed from the open fields. Hooper thus drew attention to the close
association between woodland relic hedges, and areas in which large amounts
of woodland are recorded by Domesday, in the county of Huntingdonshire
(Pollard *et al.* 1974, 90–1).

Two things stand out from this brief summary of Hooper and Pollard's
pioneering work. The first is that the two researchers were, in the 1970s,
suggesting something more complex and subtle than most subsequent users of
the 'hypothesis' have recognised. But the corollary of this is that there is an
inherent contradiction in their work between the simple 'rule of thumb'
offered by the hedge dating method, and the complex processes leading to variations in shrub content which they actually describe. A very mixed hedge
might thus have been planted with a single species, but so long ago that other
plants, even those closely associated with woodland and slow to spread beyond

it, have had time to colonise in some numbers. It might, on the other hand, represent a much younger hedge which now grows, or once grew, next to an area of woodland from which species could colonise with relative ease. It might have been planted with a range of species. Or it might represent a hedge established by managing the natural understorey of a wood during the process of colonisation, at some time before the post-medieval period. Hooper at one point acknowledged the difficulty of separating out these various forms of mixed hedge by explicitly distinguishing them from those he described as 'planted': that is, relatively young and containing varying proportions of (in the main) rapidly-colonising plants like ash or blackthorn. The complexity and ambiguity of the situation is neatly summarised in an important passage which is worth quoting in full:

> To recapitulate: the relation between relatively young planted hedges and age is thought to be largely due to simple colonisation by a fairly limited range of species, the relationship of each species with age depending on seed supply, its ability to establish, and its persistence in the hedge.
> At the other end of the range woodland relic hedges are in one sense of indeterminate age as they will be usually relics of primary woodland and have had woody cover of some type since before the first clearance of woods in the Neolithic Age. As hedges, they are usually old, much older than most planted enclosure hedges. The dating technique would group them as old hedges but it would clearly not be appropriate to try to give them a particular age using the dating method as their shrub complement will depend in part on what they started with ... (Pollard *et al.* 1974, 104).

What no subsequent writer on the subject seems to have noted is that this essential distinction, between older hedges which were mixed in character and younger ones which were dominated by hawthorn, was not in itself new. It had been made by a number of earlier writers, especially late eighteenth- and early nineteenth-century agricultural commentators. The Rev St. John Priest, for example, in the *General View of the Agriculture of the County of Buckinghamshire*, noted that the hedges of that county:

> Are of two sorts, old and new. The old fences consist chiefly of a mixture of ash, sallow, and hazel, with some whitethorn, with but few and shallow ditches ... The new fences consist of whitethorn ... (Priest 1813, 123).

John Middleton, in his volume on Middlesex, similarly contrasted the 'new quick hedges' and the older examples, which he described as 'consisting mostly of hawthorn, elm, and maple, with some black thorns, crabs, bryers and damsons' (Middleton 1813, 150). John Boys, writing about Kent, noted the difference between 'old hedges, such as Nature has formed', and the newer 'quickset hedges raised from the berries of the white thorn' (Boys 1813, 61); while in Cheshire the contrast was between the new enclosures, of 'white, or haw-thorn', and the 'ancient fences', consisting of 'hasle, alder, white or

black-thorn, witch-elm, holly, dogwood, birch &c &c' (Holland 1813, 121). In Staffordshire it was likewise reported that the 'new fences' were of whitethorn, but 'In our ancient fences many other kinds of wood are common' (Pitt 1813b, 53). The distinction between species-poor hedges of eighteenth- and nineteenth-century date, and older species-rich ones, was thus already being made more than a century and a half before Hooper and his colleagues carried out their research. What was new in their work was the suggestion that, rather than there just being a broad distinction between these two chronological categories, there were meaningful gradations of floral complexity which could be directly related to the age of a hedge. This, for good or ill, became Hooper's main legacy: the part of his work that was most appealing, and most widely accepted.

FIGURE 12.
Dogwood and field maple were considered slow colonisers by Hooper: the former in particular was a characteristic feature of older hedges.

FIGURE 13.
Spindle, another species characteristic of older hedges in the east Midlands.

Hedge 'dating' and its critics

The Hooper method was indeed quickly and immensely popular among local historians and those interested in the history of the landscape. Conservationists, too, were understandably keen to promote Hooper's ideas because they served to focus attention on the antiquity of hedges and thus provided a powerful counter-myth to that propagated by the farming industry – that they had all been established by the parliamentary enclosures of the eighteenth and nineteenth centuries and were thus of no real historical significance. The Council for the Protection of Rural England published a leaflet on the subject in 1973 (CPRE 1973). But, in general, Hooper's ideas were embraced in a remarkably uncritical manner. All of his cautions and caveats were ignored: the appeal of the 'one species, one hundred years' formula was irresistible. Ron Wilson, in *The Hedgerow Book* of 1979, typically noted: 'Until recently there was no means of finding out how old a hedge was. Today this can be done with some accuracy, to within a hundred years or so', by using the Hooper method. True, a few notes of caution were sounded: acid soils and harsh climate limited the method's effectiveness, because for it to work 'there must be enough shrubs growing'. But on the whole the 'hypothesis' was enthusiastically embraced, and one section of the book simply invited readers to 'Date Your Own Hedge' (Wilson 1979, 29). And it was not only in amateur circles that the approach was welcomed. Many academics initially embraced it in a similarly wholehearted fashion. Geoffrey Hewlett's article 'Reconstructing a Historical Landscape from Field and Documentary Evidence: Otford in Kent' appeared in the *Agricultural History Review* in 1974, and included the careful examination of 250 hedges in the parish. Hewlett concluded that 'Dr Hooper's figures are substantially correct'. Edaphic factors 'did not have an important influence on the number, as opposed to the type, of species', and in consequence most hedges could be dated to within ± 100 years with some confidence (Hewlett 1974, 95–6). Hewlett acknowledged that 'counting hedge species is not a simple answer to the local historians' prayer for new information', because hedges might on occasions be planted with more than one species, or could have been felled and replanted at some point in the past. Nevertheless, he suggested that 'the composition of a hedge is a factor in the landscape deserving of careful consideration', especially if attention was also given to such things as the size and morphology of the bank on which the hedge grew (Hewlett 1974, 96).

The hypothesis soon appeared in a number of texts by leading landscape archaeologists and historians. Christopher Taylor, for example, in his excellent *The Cambridgeshire Landscape*, noted that Hooper's method suggested that the hedge around Lopham's Hall Farm in Carlton-cum-Willingham was 'at least 900 years old, that is nearly 300 years older than the first documentary appearance of the farmstead' (Taylor 1973, 102); and that hedges at Great Shelford were created 'at least 500 years ago', while others were enclosures 'taken out of the common fields in the seventeenth century' (Taylor 1973, 142, 180).

Michael Reed, in his *Buckinghamshire* volume of the same series, published in 1979, similarly accepted that the average of 12.4 species recorded in the famous Black Hedge at Monks Risborough suggested that it 'may have been over two hundred years old when it was first mentioned in the charter of AD 903' (Reed 1979, 71). Pollard's contention that certain 'indicator species' could be used to identify hedges which had once been associated with woodland also received strong support; Helliwell's statistical analysis of survey data from hedges in Shropshire concluded that 'association analysis of the floristic data divided the sample hedgerows fairly clearly into those with several ... 'woodland' species and those with few or none' (Helliwell 1975, 71).

But by this time, however, certain aspects of the 'Hooper hypothesis' began to be examined with more scepticism. Given the widespread interest in the 'hedge dating' method among amateur and local historians it is fitting that two of the most important critiques appeared in the journal *Local Historian*. In 1978 Wendy Johnson reviewed the early literature relating to hedge planting, a particularly necessary undertaking given that certain key assumptions about the origins of hedges underpinned Hooper's approach. In particular, the fact that hedges were colonised by new species at a roughly constant rate, even if true, could only be employed as a method of dating if we could be confident that most had originally been planted with a single species. In the eighteenth and nineteenth century, certainly, hedges had usually been planted with either hawthorn or blackthorn, but even in this period additional species might be planted as timber – ash, oak, or elm; while Hooper and his colleagues had themselves noted cases where, as late as the nineteenth century, hedges themselves had been planted with more than one species (Pollard *et al.* 1974, 85). A century-old hedge which had begun life as a mixture of blackthorn and hawthorn, with a number of elm standards, would appear, according to a literal interpretation of Hooper's hypothesis, to be at least two centuries older than it really was. If it had initially been planted with a greater range of shrubs or timber, it would appear older still. Hooper believed that mixed planting had never been common, and probably limited to particular districts, such as Shropshire. But Johnson suggested that it had been common practice before *c.*1700 and produced an abundance of evidence to this effect. In his *Boke of Husbandry* of 1534, for example, Fitzherbert suggested that the 'quicksettes' for new hedges should be 'of whyte thorne and crabtree for they be beste, holye and hasell be good' (Johnson 1978, 197; Fitzherbert 1534, 53). John Norden's *Surveyor's Dialogue* of 1610 commented on the abundance of fruit trees in the hedges in Devon, Gloucestershire, Kent, Shropshire, Somerset and Worcestershire, as well as in many parts of Wales, and bemoaned the fact that they were gradually disappearing from the hedges of Middlesex and south Hertfordshire, as the modern generation failed to replace those which had grown old and died (Johnson 1978, 198–9; Norden 1609, 201) (Figure 14) (the practice nevertheless continued at least until the end of the century, to judge from the writings of Moses Cook (Cook 1676, 138). Norden – like Tusser before him, and John Evelyn and a range of writers after him – also urged that oaks, elms and ash should be planted in hedges, to grow into timber trees. Pehr Kalm, a Danish traveller who came to England in 1748, noted how in the Hertfordshire Chilterns hedges were commonly planted with a mixture of hawthorn and sloe, but that in addition the farmers 'set here and there, either at a certain distance or length from each other, or just as they please, small shoots of willows, beeches, ash, maple, lime, elm, and other leaf-trees'(Johnson 1978, 200). Although Johnson did not make the point, useful species might also be added to hedges some time *after* they had been planted. Arthur Young thus described at the end of the eighteenth century how in Hertfordshire the local shortage of firewood had 'induced the farmers to fill the old hedges every-where with oak, ash, sallow and with all sorts of plants more generally calculated for fuel than fences' (Young 1813, 49).

The second important critique to appear in the *Local Historian* came from Johnson's partner, C. J. Johnson. In an article published in 1980 he provided a timely explanation, aimed at the non-specialist, of the statistical underpin-nings of Hooper's ideas, and reminded enthusiastic hedge-daters of the statistical limits of the method, limits which Hooper himself had, indeed, stated a few years earlier: that a margin of error of 200 years either side of the indicated date needed to be left to allow 90 per cent confidence (Johnson 1980). Johnson's concern was to:

> Draw attention to the pitfalls in any over-simple approach to hedge
> dating. The technique has something to offer the historian, but at present
> there seems to be so much enthusiasm for going out and counting hedges,
> that little thought is being given to the statistical limits of the process and
> the accuracy of the result (Johnson 1980, 33).

These were both powerful *theoretical* challenges to the 'Hooper hypothesis', at least in the simple form in which this was becoming popularised. But a number of practical field studies also began to question whether there was anything very much that the historian or archaeologist could learn from the botanical examination of hedges. In the early 1980s Williams and Cunnington surveyed the hedges in Fryent Country Park in Middlesex, on either side of the Harrow and Kingsbury parish boundary (Williams and Cunnington 1985). The area had a complex history. In medieval times it had a landscape typical of the 'ancient countryside' areas of Middlesex, with small open fields and enclosed crofts interspersed with large areas of woodland. It was precisely the kind of well-wooded countryside which Hooper and his colleagues had failed to investigate in detail in their initial studies, and in which the potential prob-lems posed by an abundant source of seeds of slow-colonising, woodland plants might be expected to be encountered. The cartographic and documen-tary evidence suggested that some of the hedges in the area had been created through piecemeal enclosure, others through the assarting of woodland and management of woodland strips. Recent management of the hedges had also varied considerably, with some having been left to grow into wide strips while others had been drastically flailed back. Having sampled some 60 hedges,

FIGURE 14.
Crab apple occurs
widely in English
hedgerows. Some
examples may have
been planted there, for
early agricultural
writers recommended
planting fruit trees,
including crab apple, in
hedges.

Williams and Cunnington concluded that there was 'only a very slight, if any, relationship between hedge age and shrub diversity. The relationship of one species per hundred years did not hold'. Hedges known to have been created through assarting were more species-poor than they should have been; later hedges, on the other hand, appeared to be older than they really were. They concluded that the hedges of the area were 'too varied in origin, management and association with woodland, to be dated by the age/shrub diversity relationship'. Indeed, they suggested 'hedge management had a much greater influence on shrub diversity than the age of the hedge' (Williams and Cunnington 1985, 14, 17).

Other field surveys, however, gave modest support to some elements of Hooper and Pollard's approach whilst questioning others. In the late 1970s Alan Willmott organised a survey of all the hedges in Church Broughton in Derbyshire, a parish in which a good series of maps allowed hedges planted in the period after 1630 to be ascribed broad dates. Although it was 'rarely possible to assign an exact date of origin to hedges', most could be given a notional 'date' by assuming that they originated in the middle of a period delimited by two successive maps – usually spanning around 50 years but, in the case of the older hedges, as much as 150 (Willmot 1980, 272–3). A total of 289 hedges were 'dated' in this way. Ignoring examples located near gardens or originating as spontaneous growth beside watercourses, Willmott found that the ten woody species (other than hawthorn) which were present with a frequency of more than 5 per cent could be divided into three groups 'on the basis of their overall frequencies, and on the relationship between their frequency and the total number of woody species in each sample' (Willmot 1980, 277). Dog rose, elder and blackthorn were well represented in all the hedges, but were dominant in those containing relatively few species. Ash, oak and English elm were less common, and present with the same frequency in hedges with large or small numbers of woody species. Crab apple, holly, hazel, and maple in contrast were all relatively rare, and were most common in hedges containing large numbers of species. Willmot, following Hooper, emphasised the fact that the species in the first group were all rapid colonisers, while those in the third were slow colonisers, associated with woodland. But the species in the second group had not been singled out for particular comment by Hooper: they were, Willmott noted, all potentially timber trees, 'most likely to be planted in hedges for timber and shade' (Willmot 1980, 277).

Willmott questioned Hooper's use of regression analysis, on the grounds that it assumes that the values of the non-stochastic variable – i.e., age – is known precisely. He also rejected Hooper's use of correlation analysis, preferring instead to employ 'regression analysis using in turn the mean, the youngest possible age and the oldest possible age of each hedge as the non-stochastic variable. This procedure allows the relationship between number of species and age to be estimated, and the effect of the uncertainty of age on the relationship to be investigated'.

Analysed in this way, the Church Broughton data suggested that there was some degree of relationship between age and species content, amounting to an increase of roughly one species per century from a 'base number' of two species. The relationship was nevertheless a weak one, accounting for only about 15 per cent of the observed variation in the number of woody species. The character of the subsoil, proximity to roads, and other factors were also important (Willmott 1980, 282–4). But more importantly, while Willmott's investigations served to confirm Hooper's 'rule', if in qualified form, they also suggested that it could not be used to date hedges planted in the parish before 1630, the date of the earliest surviving map: for hedges shown on this contained only slightly more species than those established between the time it was surveyed, and the time that the next map of the parish was made in 1775 (an average of 4.64 species per 30 metres, as opposed to 4.49). Willmott suggested that this possibly indicated 'an inherent maximum number of species' able to colonise the hedges in the area (Willmott 1980, 284).

Rather similar conclusions were reached in the early 1980s by John Hall (Hall 1982). He examined 195 sample lengths (a total of 3.5 miles (5.6 km)) of hedges in Yorkshire, of which 129 could be dated, with varying degrees of confidence and accuracy, through maps or documents. Hall accepted the criticisms of Hooper's use of regression analysis which had been made by Willmott and instead examined the data using a 'one way analysis of variance' (Hall 1982, 104). He concluded that there was a meaningful relationship between age, and species number, but only in the case of relatively young hedges. Older hedges, as in the case of Church Broughton, formed a 'statistically indistinguishable group' (Hall 1982, 105). In part, he suggested, this might simply reflect the unreliable dating of many of the older hedges: documentary references often provided a date for the creation of a boundary, but not necessarily for the hedge running along it, which might have been added at a later date. 'The insurmountable problem with the method', he suggested, was 'that of identifying old hedges of accurately known date' (Hall 1982, 106).

Like both Hooper and Willmott before him, Hall noted the way that while some species were present in almost all hedges (hawthorn, elder, dog rose) others became more common in hedges of increasing age (oak, holly and sycamore) while some – most notably, hazel and maple – were 'only found in hedges planted in the fifteenth century or earlier'. Hall concluded that while recent hedges might be dated using some version of 'Hooper's rule', at least within a two-century period, 'it would seem that the limits of the method are in distinguishing groups of hedges as medieval, post-medieval and modern'. At this level of accuracy, he suggested, such things as field shapes and field names might provide as reliable a guide to the date of a hedge, although Hall sensibly noted that 'the use of species composition to identify woodland relic hedges may well be a valuable tool for landscape historians' (Hall 1982, 106–7).

Both Hall and Wilmott thus accepted certain elements of the Hooper approach while criticising others, and in particular cast doubt on the existence of any simple relationship between age and species content. Indeed, what their results tended to confirm was the basic distinction which Hooper had else-where proposed, between mixed hedges, containing an abundance of woodland species, which were usually old but effectively undatable; and 'planted' hedges, of post-medieval or recent date, which were of single-species origin but which became increasingly species-rich with age. Both studies, that is, demonstrated that while there was some relationship between age and diversity in younger ('planted') hedges, such a relationship became less clear, or disappeared entirely, with hedges planted before the seventeenth century. But in addition, both emphasised, more than Hooper had done, the extent to which environmental factors were at least as important as age in determining the species content of hedges, even relatively recent ones.

Some other studies carried out in the 1970s and early 80s, however, gave even less support to Hooper's ideas. Peter Fowler, in an article aptly entitled 'Hedged about with doubt', showed that the numbers of species recorded in hedges in the Vale of Wrington in Somerset were only poorly correlated with age. The particular *range* of species present in a hedge was a better guide to antiquity, he suggested, but factors other than age were also evidently impor-tant in generating diversity so that, in particular, hedges on roadsides generally contained more species than others (Fowler 1974). Overall, the botanical exam-ination of hedges was able to contribute little to our knowledge of landscape history. At best, the numbers of species 'indicate a relative and not necessarily an absolute time scale' (Fowler 1974, 30). Ruth Tillyard's study of the hedges of Creake in north Norfolk concluded, slightly more optimistically, that 'The Hooper method had some degree of success ... Unfortunately there were also errors: thirteen dates out of over 90 were more than a hundred years out' (Tillyard 1976, 278). Wendy Johnson, however, studied a number of hedges dated by cartographic means scattered across a wide area in the south of the same county and concluded that Hooper's rule in its simple form was 'not applicable to this area', in particular because in this anciently hedged and relatively well-wooded region younger hedges gained species at around twice the rate that Hooper had suggested – a conclusion confirmed by Sylvia Addington in a more detailed parish study carried out in Tasburgh, also in south Norfolk. Johnson concluded that 'the uncertainties in the hedge dating method (as reflected by the confidence limits around the best fit line) are so wide as to cast doubt on whether any meaningful conclusions can be drawn from the results obtained' (Johnson 1981, 187; Addington 1978, 79).

The findings from Somerset and Norfolk were echoed elsewhere. In 1979 a number of short papers were published in the journal *Hertfordshire Past and Present*, describing recent attempts at using Hooper's method. One, carried out in the parish of Clothall in the north of the county – an area of mixed chalk and boulder clay soils lying astride the division between 'planned' and 'ancient' countryside – concluded only that '. . . some of the hedges surveyed have been shown possibly to correlate with the dating theory on the basis of documentary evidence', and urged that 'care should be exercised in extrapolating this data to undocumented hedges' (Burleigh and Sawford 1979, 20). The authors suggested, in particular, that hedges arising from the management of scrub developing spontaneously on banks and baulks might well have a higher species count than Hooper's theory would predict. This observation was based on an examination of railway embankments, many of which – though less than 150 years old – 'frequently have in excess of five species per thirty yard length'. The noted Hertfordshire historian David Short similarly found a number of anomalies and discrepancies in the area around Ashwell, and recommended that the information derived from hedge surveys should be treated with caution and only used as 'part of the whole jigsaw' in studying the landscape. He noted, for example, how two hedges bounding a parliamentary enclosure road, little more than a century old, contained an average of five and six species respectively (Short 1979, 22–3). Perhaps the most interesting challenge to the Hooper hypothesis, however, was presented by a survey carried out in the parish of Aldenham, in the far south of the county. Franklyn Dulley noted, in a passage worth quoting in full, that the results:

> were paradoxical. The part of the parish on the London clay, known as 'Woodside' in the seventeenth century and still containing extensive unenclosed common in 1801, has hedges apparently nearly a century older on average than those on lighter soils to the north around the village nucleus. Worse, the only closely dated hedgerows, those subsequent to the Enclosure Act of 1801, averaged 2.7 species per 30-yard length, as against an expected 1.8 or less (Dulley 1979, 16).

He suggested that multi-species planting may have continued into the nineteenth century in the district, and also that variations in soil, farming practices and management had more effect than age on species content. Dulley, in an interesting development of Hooper's methods, drew attention to the distribution of three slow-colonising species, maple, dogwood and hazel. Within the older-settled north of the parish the three species often occurred together in hedges, rather than being scattered randomly; while in the 'Woodside' area the distribution of such hedges suggested 'a pattern of widely spaced ancient hedges with later infilling', perhaps resulting from the subdivision of small open fields carved out of the wooded uplands.

Meanwhile, on the other side of the country in the West Midlands, studies by Cameron and Pannet produced similarly discouraging results (Cameron and Pannet 1980a and b). 'The age/species relationship does not hold in Shropshire' (Cameron and Pannet 1980a, 148), in part because of a tradition of planting mixed hedges, even in the nineteenth century; and in part because the abundance of early hedges with 'woodland relic' characteristics provided a more abundant seed source than in the areas studied by Hooper and Pollard.

By the mid 1980s it was thus becoming apparent that the relationship between age, and species content, was nothing like as clear as had initially been thought. Cameron, in a masterly summary of the situation published in the journal *Biologist* in 1984, listed the wide range of factors which, in addition to age, seemed to affect the species composition of a hedge, and in passing also highlighted the important contradiction inherent in the work of Hooper and Pollard with regard to species-rich hedges. He emphasised how, according to Hooper's rule, very old hedges were species-rich because they have been colonised over a long period of time by a range of species; but how at the same time the richness of 'woodland relic' hedges 'was a consequence not so much of gradual colonisation as of the *survival* of an initially diverse array of woodland species' (Cameron 1984, 204). Cameron concluded his review with the sensible words:

> Given the many factors which can influence the species composition of hedges, it is not surprising that the initial conclusions of Hooper and Pollard have been somewhat qualified. Local variations in soils, in climate, in planting policy, and in landscape history all affect hedges to varying degrees, but the substance of their conclusion remains: that older hedges are generally richer, that this richness is in part a consequence of colonization, and that hedges made in a wooded environment retain much of their initial diversity long after the woods themselves have vanished (Cameron 1984, 207).

Of particular importance was Cameron's suggestion that although hedges could not be 'dated' in any simple or direct way by examining their composition, local historians and others could still use this kind of information in other ways: 'to identify and locate areas of one-time woodland and open fields in areas lacking documentary evidence, for example' (Cameron 1984, 208). Shortly after Cameron's article appeared, another important paper was published which in effect moved decisively towards the more flexible use of botanical information which Cameron had suggested, and which some of the earlier field studies had begun to toy with. Trevor Hussey's article 'Hedgerow

History' appeared in 1987, once again in the pages of the journal *The Local Historian* (Hussey 1987). Hussey studied the hedges of the parishes of Emmington in Oxfordshire and Napshill in Buckinghamshire but, instead of simply counting the numbers of species in sample lengths, attempted to identify clusters of hedges with similar 'profiles' – that is, similar ranges of species. The parish of Emmington lies on fertile, loamy soils in the Thames valley and was largely occupied by open fields in the medieval period. By the later Middle Ages some partial enclosure had taken place, and Hussey noted that 'The species profiles show these older hedges to be distinctive, being rich in hazel, ash and dogwood, but poor in elm. They have an average of 6.2 species'. Emmington's remaining open fields were enclosed by formal agreement in 1697, and the new hedges – which are clearly shown on a map produced the same year – had rather different profiles, with less hazel and ash but with much dogwood, maple and crab, and with an average of 4.4 species. Lastly, a number of hedges were added to the landscape in the course of the nineteenth century. These are dominated by hawthorn but also contain blackthorn, dog rose and ash, together with small quantities of elder and maple. The parish of Napshill occupied rather different terrain in the well-wooded Chiltern Hills. Here there were no early maps which could be compared with the field evidence but the hedges again fell into three broad categories. Firstly, there was a group of 'mixed species hedges with one or more woodland herbs enclosing large areas with rather sinuous outlines. They had an average of 6.5 species and their profile is distinguished by having more hazel than hawthorn, very little elder, an abundance of field maple and dogwood and some oak and beech'. Second was a group of mixed hedges with an average of 5.3 species, with more hawthorn than hazel, a high frequency of elder and holly, but little maple, beech, oak or dogwood. Lastly, Hussey identified a small group of nineteenth-century hedges which, like those in Emmington, contained hawthorn, elder, ash, dogrose, and blackthorn but not much else.

Recent developments

By the later 1980s opinions about the use of hedges as historical evidence had become polarised. Richard and Nina Muir, in their admirable book on hedges published in 1987, could dismiss almost unreservedly the whole idea of the 'Hooper hypothesis', albeit largely on *a priori* grounds, rather than on the basis of field research. There was no evidence that hedges acquired new species at an even rate; mixed planting might well have been widespread in earlier centuries; and the theory paid insufficient attention to the way that environmental factors might affect colonisation rates (Muir and Muir 1987, 53–63). They went so far as to suggest that the really interesting question was why anybody could have believed such a notion in the first place. But one part of the answer was that Hooper's approach continued to find strong support in some surprising circles. Respected archaeologists like Warwick Rodwell continued to employ it in landscape studies, albeit often with highly inconclusive results (Rodwell and

Rodwell 1993); and the method continued to find favour with some historical ecologists. Even so respected a scholar as Oliver Rackham enthusiastically endorsed Hooper's 'rule': it was 'an empirical relation which holds good over a wide range of counties; it is surprising how little influence management or geology has on the composition of an old hedge' (Rackham 1976, 167). He did, it is true, acknowledge the limitations of the approach: 'Hooper's Rule can distinguish hedges of the Enclosure Act period from those of Stuart or Tudor times or of the Middle Ages. We cannot expect it to date hedges more precisely ...' (Rackham 1986, 197). Indeed, 'It has sometimes been applied uncritically and then, when exceptions are found, has fallen into unjustified disrepute' (Rackham 1986, 202). Nevertheless, within such broad limits – and allowing for a number of exceptions, such as the planting of multi-species hedges in some districts in the nineteenth century – the Rule was a useful one which has 'told us much about the history of hedges from Northumberland and Norfolk to Devon and Kent'. Indeed, one of the sections of Rackham's chapter on hedges in his immensely popular book, *History of the Countryside*, was simply entitled: 'Why does Hooper's Rule work?' (Rackham 1986, 197). And he was not alone. Wilfrid Dowdeswell's textbook on *Hedgerows and Verges*, published in 1987, thought the approach a useful one, if used with sensible caution (Dowdeswell 1987, 33–8). The noted landscape historian John Hunter published a number of articles in which he used the rule to elucidate the history of the Essex countryside (Hunter 1993 and 1997). The number of woody species provided, he insisted, a good general guide to the age of a hedge, although he emphasised that other factors might distort this relationship. In particular, while Hooper's method worked well on the boulder clay and chalk soils of the county, it 'should be treated with reservation on certain soils; the acid Bagshot and Claygate beds, and areas of glacial outwash, encourage fewer species' (Hunter 1993, 114). And in one of the standard texts on environmental archaeology, published as late as 1999, John Evans and Terry O'Connor recommended the broad principals of the Hooper and Pollard approaches, while acknowledging the many associated problems, such as those caused by the planting of multi-species hedges (Evans and O'Connor 1999, 116–17).

With such endorsements, it is not surprising that the idea of 'hedge dating' continued to enjoy much popular support throughout the 1980s and 90s, even in its simplest and most unsubtle form. Numerous books aimed at the popular market continued to state the species number/age relationship as a matter of established fact. Streeter and Richardson's *Discovering Hedgerows*, for example, accepted Hooper's hypothesis at least as a 'rule of thumb', and used it to suggest dates of between 800 and 1000 years for an Essex hedge, the study of which formed a major feature of the book (Streeter and Richardson 1982, 102). Indeed, numerous local studies by amateur historians have continued to embrace the method right up to the present: a good example is Helen Pitchforth's *A Hidden Countryside: Discovering Ancient Tracks, Fields and Hedges*, published in 2001, which presented a particularly detailed study of the hedges of the parish of Witham in Essex (Pitchforth 2001).

The Hooper Hypothesis

One of the main reasons why the 'hypothesis' has remained so popular is its simplicity. All that is required of the practitioner is the ability to identify a relatively limited range of woody species. Indeed, it is noteworthy that few of the academic studies outlined above, and none of the more 'popular' accounts, pay any real attention to the concept of the 'woodland relic hedge', particularly in relation to the 'key indicators' among the ground flora studied by Ernest Pollard – in part, one suspects, because of the relative difficulty of identifying these plants and, more importantly, because of the relatively short 'window' during which they can be spotted with ease, before they cease to flower and become obscured by the growth of taller herbs and grasses in the late spring. Moreover, hedge 'dating', as both the present authors can confirm, is an extremely pleasant form of historical enquiry compared to archaeological fieldwalking (usually carried out in the depths of winter), or to sitting in a public records office trying to read obscure ancient documents. But, as we shall argue later, there is more to the appeal of 'hedge dating' than this. There is something peculiarly seductive about the idea that the everyday features all around us can be a direct link with the deep past, and in the concept that history and ecology can combine to give – in a particular landscape feature – a distinct sense of place. The popularity of 'hedge dating' is tied up with deeper issues, relating to the antiquity of the countryside, and to man's relationship with nature. For hedges, more than perhaps any other feature of the countryside, are both nature *and* history.

At present it would probably be fair to say that two main views on the hedgerow/history issue are current. Many landscape historians hold that the botanical examination of hedges is simply a waste of time and can provide no useful or reliable evidence, or at least can tell us nothing more than could be deduced from such things as an analysis of field shapes. Others, including some academics as well as many enthusiastic amateurs, hold that there is at least some truth in the 'Hooper hypothesis', and that counts of species in sample lengths can indeed provide a broad date for a hedge – distinguishing at the very least medieval hedges from those of Tudor and Stuart date, and both from those created by eighteenth- and nineteenth-century enclosure. Indeed, the idea that age and species content are related remains so powerful that it has influenced the details of the 1997 Hedgerow Regulations, which places the number of shrub species in a hedge as a major criteria for its protection.

Yet in a sense the quest to verify, or to disprove, the 'Hooper hypothesis' – or to find other ways in which hedges might provide useful historical data – is to miss the point. Hedges are, as we have emphasised, essential features of the landscape and their origins and development over time, and the innumerable local and regional variations which they display, are worthy of serious academic attention in their own right. In this volume we will indeed attempt to show what can be learnt from a study of hedges about the wider history of the landscape. But our main concern is simply to gain a better understanding of these important features.

CHAPTER THREE

The Context of Norfolk Hedges

Norfolk is a particularly good area in which to examine the origins and development of hedges because of the rich diversity of its landscapes, both man-made and natural. It contains a wide range of soil types, ranging from acid sands and gravels, through rich loams and alluvium, to heavy clay. It lies astride the conventional boundary between the 'planned' and the 'ancient' countryside: in the west of the county field patterns were largely created by planned post-medieval enclosure, but in the south and east they have much earlier origins. Moreover, although the county suffered badly from the intensification of agriculture in the second half of the twentieth century, in most districts substantial numbers of hedges still remain. In this chapter we will first examine the environment and landscape of the county in some detail, before discussing the broad characteristics of the region's hedges and the documentary evidence relating to their origins and past management.

The natural background: geology and climate

The character of the county's soils is largely determined by its geology, which is dominated by relatively young and fairly soft rocks. The oldest formation exposed at the surface dates from the Upper Jurassic period: Kimmeridge clay underlies the eastern part of the Fens in the west of the county and rises to the surface sporadically to form former islands, like that occupied by the villages of Hilgay and Southery. This formation also extends, as a narrow band, from Fordham to South Wootton, but is usually overlain by later deposits. Lower Cretaceous deposits are thin and likewise confined to west Norfolk. The Sandringham Sands are exposed around North and South Wootton, Bawsey, Castle Rising and Dersingham, and also further south around Downham Market. The Snettisham clay outcrops around Heacham, Snettisham, and from Ingoldisthorpe to West Newton; and Gault clay between Wereham and West Dereham and again around Shouldham and west of Narborough, as well as further north, where it changes gradually into the formation known as the Red Rock, which occurs in a narrow band between Dersingham and Hunstanton (Chatwin 1961; Funnel 1993).

All these early deposits are, however, restricted to a narrow band of country running north–south along the eastern margins of the Fens and the Wash. Far more important is the thick layer of chalk, some 420 m deep, which was laid down across most of the county in the Upper Cretaceous period. This soft white limestone forms the basic underlying geology of the county but, dipping towards the south-east, becomes buried ever deeper beneath more recent deposits. For the most part these lie 'unconformably' with the chalk, that is, their deposition did not follow immediately, but only after the rocks laid down in the intervening millennia had been eroded. They are the so-called 'Crag' deposits, a varied collection of clays, gravels and shelly sands, dating from the late Pliocene and early Pleistocene periods – between c. 3.5 and 1.6 million years ago. These form the main solid geology of east Norfolk, but are not for the most part directly exposed at the surface, being buried beneath a range of much later deposits.

Indeed, even the chalk exerts only a minor influence on the soils of Norfolk, except in the north and west of the county. During the Pleistocene a wide range of 'superficial' deposits was laid down across the county under glacial or semi-glacial conditions and, although seldom more than 50 m thick, these form the parent material for most of the county's soils. *Till* is the most extensive of these deposits and was directly deposited by ice sheets, principally of Anglian age. Three main kinds of till are found in Norfolk. Reddish till is found in a narrow band along the coastal plain of the county. It contains flints, sandstones, shales and even igneous rocks, as well as chalk. Brown till, or Norwich Brickearth, is found to the north-east of Norwich. It is a uniform and fairly stone-free brown loamy deposit, which contains occasional erratics: it is often referred to as 'North Sea Drift'. But chalky boulder clay is the most extensive and most important of these deposits, a heavy clay which blankets extensive areas in the centre and south of the county. Typically, the unweathered till is grey, calcareous and unstratified. It contains abundant pebbles and rounded fragments of chalk, as well as angular flints and occasional quartz, limestone and igneous rock fragments. The valley slopes are characterised by more loamy drift, a mixture of chalk and medium sand; or by 'head', an unsorted deposit of stones resulting from seasonal freeze-thaw action. The till surface has rounded slopes and falls gently to the east, following the dip of the underlying rocks.

Glaciofluvial sands and gravels, materials which derive from the outwash waters of ice sheets, are also of localised importance as a soil parent material. They are widely distributed in Norfolk, generally around the margins of the main areas of till. They are particularly widespread between Norwich and the Cromer Ridge, lying in a zone which separates the clayey chalky till from the loamy North Sea Drift: the prominent range of hills in the north of the county known as the Cromer–Holt ridge is capped by particularly stony outwash gravels. In south Norfolk, glaciofluvial drift also outcrops in places from beneath the chalky till on the sides of the wide valleys which drain the till plateau.

Finally, during the last ice age material eroded by the strong winds blowing near the ice fronts was widely re-deposited as *aeolian sand and silt*, although as the deposits are thin they have often been comprehensively incorporated into the underlying material. In the north and east of the county silty material of aeolian origin covers much of the Brickearth and is of great significance as a soil-forming material. Of rather different character, but similar origin, are the extensive sandy deposits in the area called Breckland in the south-west of the county.

Although deposits of glacial origin thus account for the majority of soil parent materials in Norfolk, some of post-glacial or Holocene age are also important. Peat occupies extensive areas in the southern Fens and, in the far east of the county, the Broads. It accumulated when the post-glacial rise in sea level caused freshwater flooding of the shallow Fen basin and the Broadland river valleys. Extensive areas of alluvium were also deposited by various phases of marine transgression, in the eastern Broads, the northern Fens, and along the coast to the west of Weybourne. The principal river valleys in the county likewise contain various combinations of alluvium and peat. Hedges are largely absent from the more extensive areas of these deposits, drainage dykes or ditches being the preferred form of land division. But they do sporadically occur, especially on the more restricted areas of these deposits found within minor valleys.

Geology is not, of course, the only factor which determines the character of soils. Climate is also important, and is also a direct influence on the character of the county's natural and semi-natural vegetation. Norfolk's climate is influenced, above all, by its low relief and proximity to the continent. It is little affected by the prevalent wet winds from the Atlantic, so rainfall is low and there is a greater daily and yearly temperature range than elsewhere in the UK. But there are appreciable climatic differences within the county, ranging from the drier Fens (which receive less than 600 mm of precipitation in an average year) to the wetter hills of north-west Norfolk or the Cromer–Holt ridge (which receive 700mm or more). In addition, the county's long, exposed coast-line should be noted: some species are more tolerant of salt winds than others.

The natural background: soils

The Soil Survey of England and Wales has developed a consistent and systematic basis of classification which can be used to differentiate the properties of soils. A soil *series* is the basic division, based on narrowly defined diagnostic properties largely derived from the parent material. At a county or regional level, however, the category used to define and distinguish soils is that of the *soil association*, which is a group of between two and eight co-varying series. Constituent series can display quite markedly different properties, so that an individual association can contain, in close proximity, areas of soil displaying strikingly different characteristics. Unfortunately, for most areas of Norfolk, published maps show only the distribution of associations, not series. Nevertheless, the mapped associations do provide a good general guide to soil conditions. Readers are advised to turn to Figure 15, where the rich, complex pattern of the county's soils is more clearly revealed (Hodge *et al.* 1984).

The most important clay soils found in Norfolk are those of the various

Beccles and Burlingham associations (Hodge *et al.* 1984, 117–122; 132–7). The former associations, of which Beccles 3 is the most important, mainly occupy the more level areas of the boulder clay plateau in the centre and south of the county. They are poorly draining, seasonally waterlogged soils, difficult to work but essentially fertile in character. In early prehistoric times, and again to some extent in the immediate post-Roman period, they were shunned by farmers, and in subsequent periods they were often used more for pasture than for arable. Many commons could be found here in medieval and post-medieval times, and numerous areas of woodland. The Burlingham soils, in contrast (Burlingham 1 and 3 associations), are sandier and more freely draining, and are therefore more appealing to early farmers. They generally occur on the sides of the principal valleys cutting through the clay plateau, especially in central Norfolk. Small areas of Hanslope association soils – heavy but slightly calcareous clays – also occur in places in the far south of the county, most notably in the valleys of minor tributaries draining into the Waveney. It should be noted that while the vast majority of the clay soils found in Norfolk are associated with the drift-covered plateau which occupies its centre and south, a smaller 'island' of such soils – developed over Gault clays, rather than glacial till – can be found to the west, beside the Fens, in the area to the north and east of Downham Market, principally featuring soils of the Burlingham 1 and Beccles 3 associations.

The largest areas of light, freely-draining soil are associated with the low chalk escarpment running through the west of the county, which is covered, to varying depths, with sandy, acid drift. At its foot, on the edge of the Fens, is another area of acid sands, derived not from glacial deposits but, as we have seen, from rocks laid down before the formation of the chalk, most notably the Sandringham Sands. On the slopes of the escarpment the acid drift is thin or absent, and soils of the Newmarket 2 association – coarse, sandy loams – are found, soils which are easy to work and calcareous but which leach nutrients rapidly (Hodge *et al.* 1984, 265–9). Arable land has always been relatively extensive here. Where the sands lie thicker, in contrast, on the higher ground and at the foot of the escarpment, more acidic and infertile soils occur, those of the Barrow association and the Newport 4 association, the latter especially inimical to farmers (Hodge *et al.* 1984, 107–11; 277–9). Such soils, together with those of the similar Methwold and Worlington associations, dominate the district called Breckland to the south, where they are formed in aeolian deposits. Areas of more calcareous soils (Newmarket 2 and 3 associations) also occur here, but are more restricted in area. Even at the end of eighteenth century, to judge from the county map published by William Faden in 1797, well over 40 per cent of Breckland was still heathland (Wade Martins and Williamson 1999, 13). Today, large areas are occupied by Forestry Commission plantations.

A second major area of light land extends in a patchy band from Norwich northwards to the sea. It is dominated by soils of the Newport 1 and 4 and Felthorpe associations: acid, sandy and infertile soils formed in deposits of glacio-fluvial origin. This, like Breckland, is particularly poor land, which was

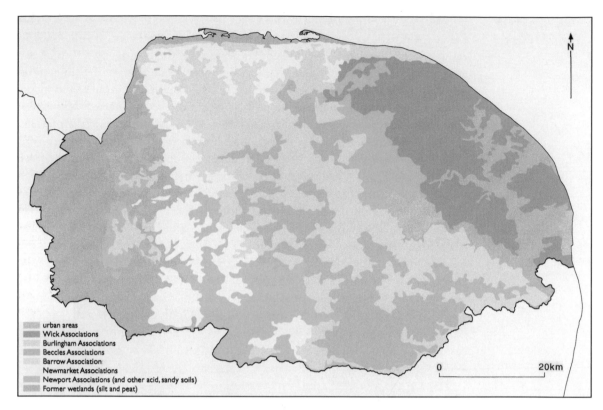

0   20km

difficult in most periods to cultivate economically. But the district also contains numerous ribbons of more loamy soil in the valleys cutting through it, and on the floors of which lush pastures and meadows were, and often still are, to be found. Moreover, the acid sands are interspersed with pockets of more loamy soils, often very extensive in area, especially in the area around Salle and Saxthorpe.

These form an eastward continuation of an extensive district of fertile loams which occupies much of eastern Norfolk, formed in thin aeolian drift overlying Brickearth or glaciofluvial sands. Areas of sandy drift occur in places but for the most part the north and east of the county are dominated by the soils of the Wick 2 and 3 associations. All are at least moderately fertile, although often prone to drought, and those of the Wick 2 association, which cover some 500 square kilometres in the area between Sheringham, Yarmouth and Cromer, are among the most easily worked and fertile soils in all England (Hodge *et al.* 1984, 346–51).

We have summarised, rather baldly, the main soil regions of Norfolk: in the process we have oversimplified, for as already noted in reality the 'associations' can include small areas of particular soil series which differ markedly in character from those around them, so that (for example) small areas of light, acid soils can be found – associated with patches of glacial sands and gravel – on the boulder clay plateau, and small areas of boulder clay in places among the sandy drift of west Norfolk.

FIGURE 15.
Norfolk: a simplified map of soils (after Hodge *et al.* 1984).

Soils have a determining effect on the species composition of hedges for three reasons. The first and most basic is that some plants are better suited to certain soils than others. Most of the plants found in the county's hedges would probably grow on any soil (hawthorn, blackthorn, ash and oak being the obvious examples) but others would be out-competed by rivals, or find it difficult to get established, in the environment of a hedge. Dogwood and guelder rose will not tolerate very acid soils; privet, spindle and wayfaring tree prefer dry, calcareous loams. Purging buckthorn is largely restricted to moist calcareous soils and will not tolerate heavy clays, but hornbeam will only thrive on these, while holly does best in neutral or mildly acidic conditions. Indeed, as Nau and Rands have pointed out, variations in soils have a major influence not only on the composition of hedges, but arguably on their diversity, with particular kinds of soil – especially leached, dry and acid sands – limiting the numbers of species which can become established, whatever a hedge's age (Nau and Rands 1975, 43). Soil type is not, of course, the only environmental characteristic favouring, or discriminating against, particular species. Norfolk's long coastline has an influence, increasing the frequency of elm and blackthorn (both notable salt-tolerant shrubs) in hedges around the northern and eastern margins of the county, and decreasing that of hazel.

The historical background: woodland and its distribution

Of equal importance in forming the character of hedges, however, are the *indirect* effects of soils and topography. As Hooper pointed out – and as the studies of Cameron, in particular, have emphasised – proximity to woodland is a significant factor in the composition of hedges, and the distribution of woodland in the county – and changes in that distribution over time – will thus have exerted an important influence on the local and regional character of hedges. So, too, will the kinds of plant growing in that woodland and thus available for colonisation, for certain shrubs – partly for environmental reasons, partly as a consequence of management practices – are found only in a small number of woods, in restricted areas of the county. Although the distribution over time of woodland was evidently the consequence of a complex range of factors, the most important was soil type. Put simply, woodland was cleared first and most comprehensively from areas of light, freely draining soils, and survived longest in areas of clay.

We are fortunate in having a large number of pollen cores which throw important light on the development of Norfolk's woodland over a very long period of time. This allows us, firstly, to ascertain something of the character of the virgin 'wildwood' in Norfolk, before any human intervention in the natural vegetation: a character largely dependent on such factors as soils, climate, time of arrival and availability of symbiotic mychorrhizal fungi. Later arrivals such as hornbeam (*Carpinus betulus*) took longer to reach their maximum abundance because they had to displace existing woody vegetation rather than simply colonising bare ground, and were thus comparatively poorly represented. Small-leaved lime (*Tilia cordata*) was probably the most common dry land tree species in Norfolk, with hazel (*Corylus avellana*), pendunculate oak (*Quercus robur*), ash (*Fraxinus excelsior*) and elm (both wych elm, *Ulmus glabra*, and the East Anglian or smooth-leafed elm, *Ulmus carpinifolia*) also common.

More importantly, the evidence of pollen analysis allows us to chart the impact of man on the extent and distribution of woodland, and on the relative abundance of species within it, although problems in dating many pollen cores, and uncertainty about how wide an area the pollen in any particular deposit was derived from, mean that this kind of evidence has to be interpreted with caution. The earliest clearances were probably made by mesolithic hunter-gatherers from about 6500 BP, but the first major impact came with the adoption of farming during the Neolithic, and with its increasing importance in the Bronze Age, particularly on the lighter soils of the north-west of the county and in Breckland. Some woodland may have been deliberately cleared but most probably degenerated through the pressure of grazing, leading to the formation of the heaths which, until the nineteenth and twentieth century, covered extensive areas of the county (Figure 16). A good example of this change is seen in the case of the Bronze Age barrow at Bawsey (Murphy 1993, 20). Soil sealed beneath the barrow shows a surrounding landscape of lime/hazel woodland. However, after the mound's construction the area became dominated by more open heathland.

By the Iron Age (*c.*2800–1960 BP) settlement and cultivation were widespread even on the clay soils in the centre and south of the county although the extent of clearance seems to have varied considerably from area to area. Around Silfield near Wymondham, for example, there was virtually no tree cover by the later Iron Age yet at Scole, in the valley of the Waveney, woody *taxa* percentages of around 40 per cent have been recorded around this time. Nevertheless, the extent of settlements discovered by archaeological surveys leave little doubt that the later Iron Age and Roman periods witnessed large-scale destruction of woodland (Rogerson 1995; Davison 1990). Pollen cores from Diss Mere, for example, show that the area under woodland decreased markedly in the period 2500–1500 years BP (Peglar *et al.* 1989). Of particular note is the apparent *increase* in the frequency of hornbeam (*Carpinus betulus*), which was attributed by the researchers to the removal of competitors but may in fact reflect the natural expansion of this species – a late coloniser, as we have seen – in the local woodland, or simply result from the fact that, being a tree most suited to the heaviest land, hornbeam tended to survive better than other species as the frontiers of cultivation expanded.

The end of the Roman period was associated with a marked decline in population and a retrenchment of settlement, involving the abandonment of much of the heavier land. In Fransham in central Norfolk, for example, a detailed archaeological survey by Andrew Rogerson revealed that the 11 sites occupied in Romano-British times had declined to 5 by the early Saxon period (Rogerson 1995), while the number of sites in Hales, Loddon and Heckingham in the south-east of the county was similarly reduced, from 15 to 4 (Davison 1990). However, this contraction of settlement does not seem to have been accompanied by the wholesale return of woodland. Localised regeneration certainly occurred: a number of finds of material of prehistoric and Roman date have been made within areas known to have been occupied by woodland in medieval and post-medieval times, and place-name evidence suggests that some areas later occupied by heathland were wooded in Anglo-Saxon times, probably as a result of regeneration over land cleared in earlier centuries. But for the most part, pollen cores suggest an increase in the area under *pasture* as the area under arable cultivation contracted, although it should be remembered that pollen sites tend to be on river valleys, and these might not record the changing vegetation patterns on higher ground (Barnes 2003, 76–8). This is important because, as we move into the Saxon period and have more diverse sources of evidence at our disposal, it is clear that topography, as well as soils, was a major factor in the distribution of woodland.

Domesday Book shows that the distribution of woodland in Norfolk was strongly structured (Figure 17). On the light soils of Breckland, north-west and north-east Norfolk there was relatively little woodland, and in some places no woodland at all. Instead, the largest areas of woodland were concentrated in a 'wooded crescent' running from Bungay in the south-east, through Attleborough and East Dereham in the centre of the county, and then back round to the area around Cromer. This distribution parallels, in broad terms, the pattern displayed by place-names featuring elements relating to woodland or its clearance – *ley, feld, wudu* and the like – which were probably coined at various times during the previous three centuries (although Domesday fails to mirror a similar concentration of such names on the edge of the Broadland marshes: Williamson 1993, 59–63, 113–15; Barnes 2003). The 'crescent' is related to a large extent to the character of the soils: it corresponds to areas of heavy plateau clay in the south and centre of the county, and to areas of poor, acid gravel in the north. However, other areas of equally heavy clay, especially in the far south-east of the county, were less markedly wooded, while many areas of poor acid gravel were apparently devoid of significant stands of woodland by the time of Domesday. The distribution is, in fact, also a consequence of *topography*. The woodland crescent corresponds closely to the major watershed which runs in a broad arc through the centre of the county, between rivers draining eastwards into the Norfolk Broads, and those draining to the north and west (Williamson 1993, 14–19; 114). And at a more local scale, both Domesday Book and place-name evidence suggest that the largest areas of woodland were on interfluves and watersheds between the principal drainage basins. Such a pattern reflects the fact that from the Iron Age through to Saxon times the main settlements, and the principal arable areas, tended to be located within the larger valleys, where good supplies of running water were found, together with well-watered pastures for livestock and the most fertile and easily cultivated soils. The high interfluves between the principal valleys, in contrast, were not only occupied by the heaviest clays and the poorest sands: they also

lacked dependable supplies of water. Such areas thus tended to be colonised at a relatively late date, and to be used less intensively by early farmers. Woodland therefore tended to survive better here into the historic period (Williamson 2003, 38–40; Everitt 1977).

Most of the woodland recorded in Domesday – and, in all probability, the majority of woodland in previous centuries – consisted of 'wood-pasture', that is, areas in which there were abundant trees but not (as in most later woods) a managed understorey. Instead, shrubs, grass and other herbage grew beneath the trees, and were regularly grazed by livestock (Figure 18) (Rackham 1976, 135–51). In the period between the tenth and the thirteenth centuries, as population increased, much of this woodland was destroyed. It was cleared to make way for arable land or, if used as common grazing, it gradually degenerated to open pasture. The speed with which destruction and degeneration occurred – and how this varied from place to place, and on different soil types – remains unknown: as we shall see, the evidence of hedges may throw some light on this issue. But some areas of woodland were enclosed and preserved by manorial lords, in the form of deer parks – in effect, private wood-pastures – or as managed woods, in which an understorey composed of coppice stools was cut on a rotation of around five to ten years, in order to produce a regular crop of 'poles' suitable for firewood and a host of other uses (Figure 19) (Rackham 1976, 18; 79–83). By the high Middle Ages the majority of such woodland could be found on the clays, in the centre and the south of the county (Rackham 1986). Woodland tended to survive best on the central and southern sections of the 'crescent', and especially towards the margins of the

FIGURE 16.
Salthouse Heath in north Norfolk. Most heaths were first deforested in prehistoric times, although some carried woodland into the Middle Ages.

FIGURE 17.
The distribution of the principal areas of woodland in Norfolk in late Saxon times, as recorded in Domesday Book. Most woodland was concentrated in a broad arc running through the centre of the county, corresponding with the main watershed between rivers draining east, into the Broadland marshes, and those draining north and west.

interfluves – perhaps a consequence of decisions by early medieval landowners to preserve this resource in locations which limited the distance which wood and timber had to be transported down rutted clay tracks (Witney 1990).

There may have been some limited increase in the area under woodland during the period of demographic decline associated with the Black Death in the later fourteenth and fifteenth centuries, but this did not change its overall distribution. Most woodland continued to be concentrated on the clays, with only limited stands on the lighter soils. More significant changes occurred in the course of the eighteenth and nineteenth centuries, however. The rise of large landed estates and the spread of enclosure encouraged the establishment of new areas of woodland and plantation across extensive areas of northern and western Norfolk, often on land formerly occupied by heaths and other commons.

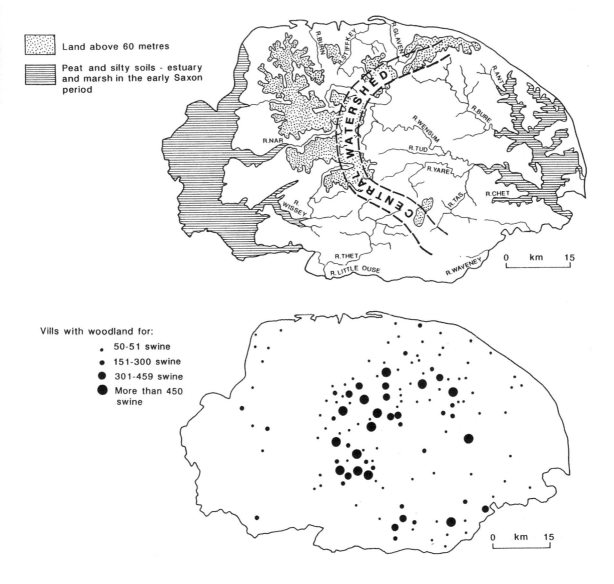

At the same time, improvements in land drainage and a fashionable hostility to traditional forms of woodland management led to the grubbing up of many ancient woods, especially small groves and copses, on the claylands.

As we have seen, pollen evidence suggests that the uncleared virgin 'wildwood' of Norfolk largely consisted of a mixture of small-leafed lime, hazel, pendunculate oak, ash and elm; subsequent changes in woodland composition, such as the increasing importance of hornbeam, are in part the result of human influence, in part the result of natural developments. In both the original 'wildwood', and in the more fragmented stands of managed woodland and wood-pasture that succeeded it, the particular balance of species varied from place to place. Hornbeam is thus a prominent feature of the ancient woods of the south Norfolk claylands but is rare elsewhere; lime is a characteristic feature of north-central Norfolk woods such as Hockering, Briston and Swanton Novers Great Wood; while sessile oak is restricted to woods on acid gravels in the north and north-east of the county, notably Holt Wood and Edgefield Little Wood. Such variations will potentially have contributed to the diversity of species content exhibited by Norfolk's hedges.

The historical background: farming and enclosure

Soils and topography were thus important influences on the distribution and character of Norfolk's woodland over the ages, and thus on the character of the county's hedges. They also had other indirect effects. They were a major influence on the character of local farming systems, and these in turn were intimately associated with variations in the progress of enclosure, and thus the speed with, and the extent to which, hedges became established in the landscape (Figure 20).

The agricultural history of this large county is again complex but we can begin by making a broad distinction between the light, freely draining and often acid soils found mainly in the north and west, and the clays of the south and centre (Wade Martins and Williamson 1999, 7–28). In medieval times, and through until the eighteenth century, the former were champion areas of 'sheep-corn husbandry', with extensive areas of unhedged arable open fields and much heathland (Wade-Martins and Williamson 1999, 7–13; Postgate 1973). In some places the numerous strips of individual farmers were widely and relatively evenly distributed through the territory of the vill, usually they were more clustered, but everywhere the organisation of arable was tightly controlled by manorial courts. Nutrients were rapidly leached from these porous soils and fertility could only be maintained by grazing large flocks of sheep on the heaths or harvest residues by day, and closely folding them on the arable by night, when it lay fallow or before the spring sowing. In most parishes, by the late Middle Ages, foldcourses operated: the close folding was a manorial monopoly. While the tenants might benefit from the dung dropped as the sheep roamed over the fallows they could only enjoy the intensive night-folding in return for a cash payment, and they were obliged to lend their own sheep to the manorial flock. In post-medieval times the character of the foldcourse gradually changed. Instead of being used in the traditional manner, to ensure that a disproportionate amount of manure came to the demesne arable, landlords now used it as a way of monopolising the grazing afforded by the crop residues and fallow weeds of the open fields. Tenants' sheep were now excluded from large commercial flocks and the foldcourse became, in effect, a way of running sheep over other people's land (Allison 1957; Bailey 1989 and 1990).

The prevalence of foldcourses across the light lands of western and northern Norfolk was in part a manifestation of the poor, easily leached character of the local soils, and the consequent importance of controlling supplies of manure. But it also reflected the fact that these were, in general, highly manorialised districts in the Middle Ages, in which the power of lords was strong. Such relatively marginal environments, moreover, in common with most areas of sheep-and-corn farming in England, continued to be dominated by large landed estates throughout the post-medieval period. By the nineteenth century, families like the Cokes of Holkham owned vast quantities of land and controlled the farming and social life of great swathes of the district.

The existence of foldcourses tended to limit the progress of early enclosure by 'piecemeal' methods, because landowners jealously guarded the rights of the manorial flocks to range freely over the fields during the fallow season (Wade Martins and Williamson 1999, 34–6). At Ashill in Breckland undated mid eighteenth-century documents describe the lord of the manor's claim that the farmers deliberately planted crops in positions that prevented the sheep moving through the fields, 'By which Means the sheeps feed hath been and still is nearly precarious'. The farmers wanted to grow turnips and clover in the fallow fields,

> which in this parish are become a great improvement and infact Sir Henry Bedingfield descendants and his daughter who lived near the said parish and were well acquainted with the customs of the said manor did for more than 40 years ackuiesse and no way oppose the landowners inclosing and sowing the said new enclosures with turnips' (NRO Pete Box 17/1).

Only as manorial lords were persuaded of the value of the new crops, and especially as the price of cereal crops began to rise in the second half of the eighteenth century, were the extensive open fields enclosed, allowing farmers to follow whatever course of cropping they saw fit. But not only was the arable land extensively reorganised and enclosed in the agricultural revolution period. Under the new systems of husbandry the heaths and sheepwalks were no longer needed as 'nutrient reservoirs', and could now be enclosed and reclaimed.

The light lands thus have a relatively short enclosure history. Early seventeenth-century maps, such as that made of North Creake in 1624, show some hedges surrounding piecemeal enclosures close to villages (NRO

FIGURE 18.
Staverton Park, Suffolk:
one of the few
remaining areas of
ancient wood-pasture
in East Anglia.

Diocesan T123A) (Figure 21). In some parishes a proportion of the roads, and sections of parish boundary, might also be hedged. But for the most part these sheep-and-corn landscapes remained open until the eighteenth century, when large estates began to enclose those parishes in which they were the monopoly landowners. Parishes with more complicated patterns of ownership, in contrast, were mainly enclosed by parliamentary acts in the course of the later eighteenth and early nineteenth centuries.

So far we have discussed the light land, sheep-corn districts of Norfolk as if they were a single, undifferentiated type of countryside. But there are, in particular, important differences between those lying in the north-west of the county – the area described as the 'Good Sands' by the eighteenth-century agriculturalist Arthur Young – on the one hand; and Breckland, and the heath-lands to the north of Norwich, on the other. In the north-west, areas of calcareous soil are relatively extensive, and the area under arable cultivation in the Middle Ages was correspondingly large. Moreover, the sandy drift occupying the higher ground was generally thin: through intensive marling the heaths and sheepwalks could be reclaimed with comparative ease, and they largely disappeared in the course of the eighteenth and nineteenth centuries. Breckland, and the heathlands to the north of Norwich, were more hostile environments, with much less open-field land and much more heath (Figure 22). The worst parts of Breckland were almost like a desert: when exposed to the wind by excessive rabbit grazing or cultivation the sand was liable to blow, and mobile dunes might form. William Gilpin, visiting the area in the 1760s, described 'sand, and scattered gravel, without the least vegetation; a mere African desert.' He continued:

> In many places we saw the sand even driven into ridges; and the road totally covered; which indeed everywhere was so deep, and heavy, that four horses, which we were obliged to take, could scarce in the slowest pace, drag us through it. It was a little surprizing to find such a piece of *absolute desert* almost in the heart of England. To us it was a novel idea. We had not even heard of it (Gilpin 1809, 28–9).

As grain prices rose to dizzy heights during the Napoleonic Wars, even the harshest heaths were enclosed. But in the course of the nineteenth century, and especially during the agricultural depression of the late nineteenth and early twentieth centuries, they were often abandoned once more and in the 1920s and 30s many came to be planted with conifer plantations by the Forestry Commission (Wade Martins and Williamson 1999, 192–3).

The other main landscape regions in the county – the loams of the north-east and the claylands in the south and centre – have longer and more complex enclosure histories. The claylands were extensively settled by late prehistoric times and it is possible that in some places the essential, underlying framework of the landscape dates back to this period. Certainly, in a number of places the boundary pattern displays a remarkably ordered and regular form, resembling in plan rather wavy brickwork, very similar to the 'co-axial' field systems of prehistoric date found in the form of earthworks or tumbled walls in some

FIGURE 19.
Old hazel coppice stools in woods at South Burlingham, Norfolk.

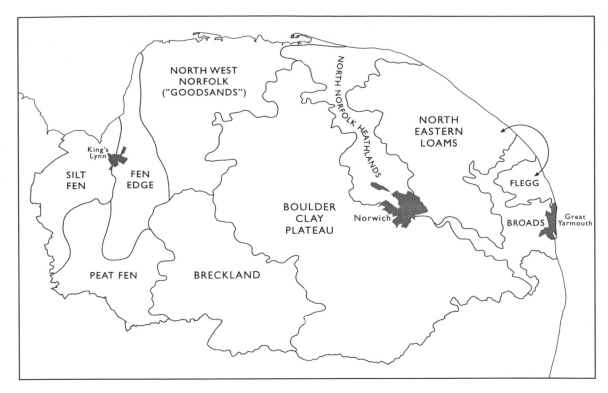

upland and chalkland areas of England. In the area around Scole and
Dickleburgh one such pattern appears to be slighted by the Roman Pye Road,
the modern A140: the road appears to slice through the fields in a way
analagous to a modern bypass (Williamson 1998b). But even if the clayland
landscape does, in some places, have its origins in prehistoric times, few of the
boundaries here are likely to be of this kind of antiquity, and even fewer of
the hedges. Many are probably the consequence of the later 'infilling' of an
originally much sparser network of lanes and boundaries, related to the division and management of woodland and grazing on the drift-covered plateaux
above major valleys. More importantly, in the course of the late Saxon and
early medieval periods open fields seem to have developed within these ancient
frameworks, presumably through the repeated subdivision of land between co-
heirs. Piecemeal enclosure from the fifteenth century seldom re-established
hedged boundaries along the original lines of division: instead, it served to
perpetuate the general orientation, rather than the particular details, of these
ancient landscapes.

Open fields were, indeed, much more widespread on the clay soils of
Norfolk in the early Middle Ages than some writers have asserted (Skipper
1989). Most of the lighter clays of the Burlingham associations – on the gently
sloping sides of the principal valleys – seem to have been occupied by subdivided arable. But open fields could also be found in many places on the heavier
plateau soils of the Beccles 3 association, albeit here often intermixed with areas
of woodland, parks and commons, together with some small hedged closes

The map contains the labels: *The Clay Pit*, *Angral Way*, *Mill Furlong*.

FIGURE 21.
Part of a map of North
Creake, surveyed in
1624, showing the
largely hedgeless
landscape typical of the
'Good Sands' region of
north-west Norfolk.
Some piecemeal
enclosure has taken
place in the areas
closest to the village,
but most of the parish
remains as open fields,
divided into a plethora
of unhedged strips.

held in severalty (Figure 23). Commons in particular were a prominent feature, extending over many hectares of the more acidic, or level and waterlogged, areas (Figure 24). Most were originally wooded, but gradually lost their trees through intensive grazing pressure (Barnes 2003, 135–43). From the eleventh century they became major foci for settlement, as farms drifted away from older late Saxon settlement sites which are today often marked by isolated churches (Wade-Martins 1980; Rogerson 1995; Davison 1990).

During the fifteenth, sixteenth and seventeenth centuries the clayland open fields underwent steady piecemeal enclosure. Informal enclosure was an easier matter here than on the light, sheep-corn lands, in part because of the absence of foldcourses in these more fertile and less landlord-dominated lands: although large estates certainly existed on the clays, such as those based on Kimberley or Raveningham, much of the land here, even in the nineteenth century, was in the hands of small proprietors or minor gentry, or else formed the outlying fragments of large estates which were based elsewhere. Enclosure was partly associated with an expansion of permanent grassland as the area ceased to be one of mainly arable farming and came to specialise in bullock fattening and dairying, although wheat continued to be an important

FIGURE 22.
William Faden's map
of Norfolk, published
in 1797, shows that vast
areas of Breckland still
consisted of
unreclaimed heathland
and arable open fields.

commodity (Holderness 1985). In the words of one sixteenth-century writer, the 'woodland and pasture' part of Norfolk was 'sustayned cheefly by graseinge, by Dayries and rearinge of Cattell, yett it is able both to maintayne itself with Corne and to afforde an overplus to their neighboures in Suffolk' (Smith 1974, 4).

By the start of the eighteenth century open fields had almost completely disappeared and the area was characterised by enclosed fields varying widely in size and shape. But vast areas of greens and commons remained. These could not easily be enclosed by informal, piecemeal methods and generally survived until the period around 1800 when, during the period of high prices during the Napoleonic Wars, they were removed wholesale by parliamentary enclosure acts. Today they can still often be recognised in the landscape as islands of rectilinear fields (and roads) surrounded by fields with more sinuous, irregular boundaries.

*The Context of
Norfolk Hedges*

FIGURE 23.
Thomas Waterman's
map of Morley,
surveyed in 1624, shows
many of the features
which were
characteristic of the
landscape of the
Norfolk claylands in
the early modern
period: damp
commons, woodland,
irregular open fields
and pasture closes.

In part the disappearance of the commons was associated with another major shift in the economy of the claylands. In the later eighteenth century – as part of the general intensification of arable agriculture which occurred at this time across the east of England – they ceased to be an area geared to cattle farming and came instead to specialise in cereal production. Land was under-drained on a large scale and, more importantly, the existing pattern of field boundaries was often extensively altered, to make it more suitable for arable farming – a development which, as we have seen, was shared by many areas of 'ancient countryside' in this period (Wade Martins and Williamson 1999, 61–9). Some hedges were removed, to make larger fields; some were grubbed out and replanted with hawthorn; many were straightened. The extent of these changes was greatest on the land of large estates but, as we shall see, took place to some extent everywhere.

The development of the landscape on the loams of north-east Norfolk falls, in many ways, between that of the light lands of the north and west, and the clays in the centre and south of the county. Like the claylands, this was a district of extensive if irregular open fields, and of numerous commons surrounded by ribbons of farms and cottages (Campbell 1981, 26–30). And here, too, the absence of foldcourses and the weakness of manorial authority allowed the steady and early removal of open arable by piecemeal enclosure. Yet there was much less woodland than on the clays by medieval times, and fewer deer parks. Moreover, in spite of the extent of piecemeal enclosure the continuing importance of arable as opposed to pasture farming on these relatively light soils ensured that rather more open-field land survived here into the nineteenth century, to be removed – together with many areas of common grazing – by parliamentary enclosure. Nevertheless, by and large the landscape history of the two districts is broadly comparable, and contrasts with that of the light lands of west Norfolk.

This brief account has concentrated on the largest landscape regions in the county, but there were others, smaller but no less distinctive. To the north of Norwich, for example, and extending northwards to the sea, lies a narrow band of poor acid soils, a kind of Breckland in miniature. Here, open fields and heaths remained extensive until the nineteenth century, and modern conifer plantations now dominate the landscape.

Norfolk thus has a complex enclosure history and one which is still not fully elucidated. This is largely because, while enclosure achieved through parliamentary acts and similar methods in the eighteenth and nineteenth centuries is relatively well documented, much less is known of the chronology or extent of early piecemeal enclosure – and thus of the extent of open fields in medieval times on the clays and loams in the south and east of the county. Indeed, the evidence provided by the composition of hedges could, potentially, add to our understanding of these matters. But we have in addition another technique at our disposal. As already noted, piecemeal enclosure produces distinctive field patterns featuring numerous small kinks and dog-legs, and gently curving boundaries – and we can use these to map its incidence across the county. And

FIGURE 24.
This extract from William Faden's county map of 1797 shows the extensive areas of common grazing which still survived on the south Norfolk claylands at the end of the eighteenth century. Almost all were enclosed by parliamentary act during the following two decades.

post-medieval *general* enclosure, by parliamentary act or otherwise, also produced diagnostic shapes, in the form of markedly rectilinear boundary patterns. As Figure 25 shows, the two types of field pattern together account for the overwhelming majority of enclosed land in Norfolk, suggesting that most of the county was once occupied by open fields or commons. Most field boundaries must, in consequence, date from the period between the fifteenth century, when enclosure began in earnest, and the mid nineteenth, when the last enclosures by parliamentary act took place.

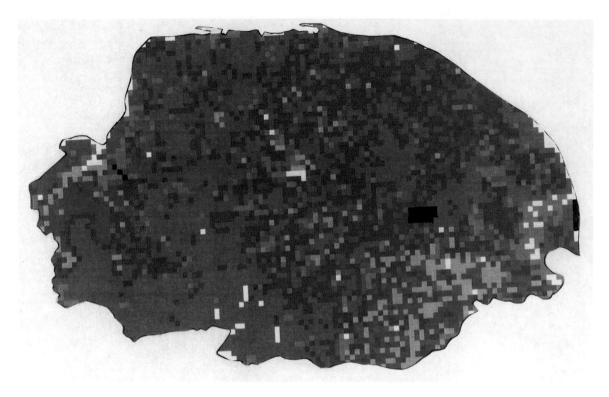

In many parts of Norfolk the field pattern underwent profound simplification – and in some places, virtual destruction – in the second half of the twentieth century. Around 500 miles (805 km) of hedgerow were grubbed out in the county each year from 1946 to 1955, rising to around 2,400 miles (3,864 km) per year by 1962, and reaching 3,500 miles (5,635 km) over the next four years. By 1970 the rate had dropped to around 2,000 miles (3,220 km) a year (Baird and Tarrant 1970), and declined more gradually through the 1970s and 80s. But an appalling amount of damage had by now been done to the historic landscape. As in other areas of England, destruction was greatest in the early-enclosed districts, especially on the claylands where, in some parishes, very few hedges now remain. In the north and west, in contrast, the rate of removal was much less, in part because the large rectilinear fields created here by late enclosure were better suited to large modern machines, in part because much of the land is in the hands of large estates.

Hedges: composition, planting and management

No fewer than 61 different species of shrub occur in Norfolk hedges, including the various species of rose, elm, and willow (Table 1), although many are present in only a very tiny proportion of hedges. The majority are natives, although old introductions like sweet chestnut and sycamore are encountered and, in restricted areas, more exotic plants like the Duke of Argyll's Tea Plant and lilac. There is remarkably little direct documentary evidence for the

FIGURE 25.

Table 1. Species present in Norfolk hedges

The varying importance within Norfolk of the three main forms of enclosure, as reflected in the modern landscape. Blue represents areas dominated by rectilinear field patterns, indicative of planned general enclosure, mostly by parliamentary act in the eighteenth and nineteenth centuries. Red represents areas mainly characterised by early piecemeal enclosure. The white areas are dominated by irregular field patterns, apparently resulting from direct enclosure from the 'waste'. Mapped by kilometre square: where none of these patterns is clearly dominant, this is indicated by the appropriate mixture of colours (e.g., purple represents areas in which both piecemeal enclosure, and planned enclosure, are prominent). Yellow represents areas still devoid of field boundaries, mainly heaths and areas of coastal sand.

Species present in more than 50 per cent of Norfolk hedges

Ash (*Fraxinus excelsior*)
Blackthorn (*Prunus spinosa*)
Elder (*Sambucus nigra*)
Elm, East Anglian (*Ulmus carpinifolia*)

Hawthorn (*Crataegus monogyna*)
Rose *Rosa sp.* *
Oak, pendunculate (*Quercus robur*)

* Different species were not systematically distinguished by the survey, but mostly dogrose, *Rosa canina*, with some field rose (*Rosa arvensis*), sweet briar (*Rosa rubiginosa*) and burnet rose (*Rosa pimpinellifolia*)

Species present in 10–50 per cent of Norfolk hedges

Hazel (*Corylus avellana*)
Holly (*Ilex aquifolium*)
Sycamore (*Acer pseudoplatanus*)

Crab apple (*Malus sylvestris*)
Dogwood (*Cornus sanguinea*)
Maple (*Acer campestris*)

Species present in less than 10 per cent of Norfolk hedges

Alder (*Alnus glutinosa*)
Apple (*Malus domestica*)
Aspen (*Populus tremula*)
Beech (*Fagus sylvatica*)
Barberry (*Berberis vulgaris*)
Birch (*Betula pendula*)
Broom (*Cytisus scoparius*)
Buckthorn, alder (*Frangula alnus*)
Buckthorn, purging (*Rhamnus cathartica*)
Bullace (*Prunus insititia*)
Cherry plum (*Prunus cersifera*)
Cherry, wild (*Prunus avium*)
Cherry, bird (*Prunus padus*)
Cypress (*Chamaecyparis sp.*)
Damson (*Prunus domestica*)
Duke of Argyll's Tea Plant (*Lycium barbarum*)
Elm, English (*Ulmus procera*)
Elm, wych (*Ulmus glabra*)
Gorse (*Ulex europaeus*)
Gooseberry (*Ribes uva-crispa*)
Guelder rose (*Viburnum opulus*)
Hornbeam (*Carpinus betulus*)
Horse chestnut (*Aesculus hippocastanum*)
Lilac (*Syringa vulgaris*)

Laurel (*Prunus laurocerasus*)
Lime (*Tilia X vulgaris*)
Lime, small-leafed (*Tilia cordata*)
Midland hawthorn (*Crataegus oxycanthoides*)
Oak, sessile (*Quercus petraea*)
Oregon grape (*Mahonia aquifolium*)
Plum, domestic (*Prunus domestica*)
Poplar, black (*Populus nigra*)
Poplar, white (*Populus alba*)
Privet, wild (*Ligustrum vulgare*)
Privet, garden (*Ligustrum ovafolium*)
Rowan (*Sorbus aucuparia*)
Scots pine (*Pinus sylvestris*)
Snowberry (*Symphoricarpos rivularis*)
Spindle (*Euonymus europaeus*)
Spurge laurel (*Daphne laureola*)
Sweet chestnut (*Castanea sativa*)
Whitebeam (*Sorbus aria*)
Wild pear (*Pyrus communis*)
Wild service (*Sorbus torminalis*)
Willow, crack (*Salix fragilis*)†
Willow, white (*Salix alba*)†
Willow, goat (*Salix caprea*)†
Yew (*Taxus baccata*)

† The various species of willow were not systematically distinguished by the survey, nor the two species of oak. In addition, the various forms of *Prunus* were not always identified accurately. These facts should be born in mind in the discussion that follows.

species originally planted in Norfolk hedges, at least in the period before *c*.1700. Parliamentary enclosure acts for the county usually stipulate the plantings of 'quicks' or 'quicksets', evidently meaning hawthorn to judge from the overwhelming dominance of this plant in hedges of this period, although blackthorn, or hawthorn/blackthorn mixtures, were also used (Figures 26 and 27).

Estate accounts from the eighteenth and nineteenth centuries also suggest that vast quantities of hawthorn were purchased by landowners involved in enclosure and reclamation schemes. Nevertheless, even in this period the documentary evidence suggests that mixed hedges were sometimes planted. In 1779, when new enclosures on Tottington Heath were being made by the Merton estate, a memorandum noted that 'between every two or three plaits of Quick to put in a plant of Holley; and to sow or plant Sweet Briar, above and below the layer'. The latter is a surprising inclusion, perhaps made for aesthetic rather than practical reasons. A further memorandum noted: 'And on the Flat of the Opposite Side of the Ditch to plant three Rows of Holley to form a future Holley fence', indicating that some pure holly hedges were also being established at this time (NRO WLS LXI/II). Perhaps the particularly arid conditions on Tottington Heath encouraged such experimentation – parts of Breckland were also divided, as we shall see, by hedges of Scots pine in this period. But there are hints of mixed planting elsewhere. Randall Burroughs of Wymondham, on the south Norfolk claylands, who kept a farming journal in the 1790s, refers on several occasions to the planting of new hedges with thorns '*and spring*', perhaps suggesting a mixture of hawthorn and ash (Wade Martins and Williamson 1996, 96). On the other hand, Nathaniel Kent, describing the process of piecemeal enclosure as practised around this time in north-east Norfolk, described how 'Whenever a person can get four or five acres together, he plants a *whitethorn* hedge around it' (Kent 1796, 72; our italics), although his contemporary William Marshall also noted the occasional use of gorse hedges on the poorer soils of this district (Marshall 1787, 110).

Moving earlier than *c*.1700 there is little documentary evidence for the choice of hedging plants. Documents recording the establishment of new hedges normally refer in vague terms to 'laye' or 'layer', or 'springs'. When the deer park at Gimmingham in north Norfolk was subdivided into fields in the 1550s, several of the closes were specifically enclosed with 'a dyche of quykke sett', a term which already, in all probability, meant hawthorn. The same document also, however, makes reference to some of the new hedges being composed of 'thornz and fensyng stuffe', again perhaps suggesting mixed planting (Hoare 1918). At Forncett in 1378, however, men were paid for 'pulling plants of thorn and ash to put on one ditch from the south of the manor to the churchyard' (Davenport 1967), while at Congham in the 1590s protesters destroyed a hedge of 'young ashes' planted around an illegal enclosure (PRO: TNA E134/40 & 41 Eliz/Mich 21). An extent of Snetterton from 1516 refers to an elm hedge, although whether it had been planted as such is again unclear: as we shall see, elm has a tendency to invade a hedge through suckering, displacing other species present (Davison 1973, 349). Perhaps the most interesting information comes from the detailed accounts maintained by the Stiffkey estate in north Norfolk in the late sixteenth century. There are a number of references to hedging materials, and while most are fairly vague – to the purchase of '400 and a quarter of lawre' in September 1587, for example – some are more explicit. There are references to the purchase of a thousand 'allder lawre' in 1590, and of 11,000 'whightthorne lawer' in 1592. In the same year 2,100 'blackthorne and 600 allder lawer' were purchased, possibly indicating the planting of a mixed hedge: so too might the purchase in 1592 to '1,000 of whight thorne and 1000 of black thorne'. More explicit is the reference in December 1592 to '2 thousand of lawer bought by Tayler whereof half a thowsand was blackthorn'. These plants were evidently for a single mixed hedge, for a subsequent entry in the accounts refers to '1500 lawer to the same close' (Bailiff accounts, code FE, Bacon archive, University of East Anglia).

Taken at face value the documentary evidence – such as it is – suggests that single-species planting of hawthorn was common in the county by the sixteenth century, but that some planting of mixed hawthorn/blackthorn, blackthorn/alder and hawthorn/ash hedges also took place, while other species were customarily set as timber when hedges were planted. There is some evidence, also, for the planting of ash and perhaps elm hedges. By the later eighteenth century single-species hawthorn planting was standard, but even then limited multi-species planting occasionally occurred, and additional species, intended to develop into timber trees, were also included. We would emphasise, however, that by its very nature such documentary evidence reflects the activities of large landowners – manorial lords, and the owners of large estates. It is perfectly possible, indeed probable that among small peasant proprietors different methods were adopted. In this context, it is perhaps worth considering how many of the commoner plants found in Norfolk hedges (Table 1) might have been intentionally planted, and what proportion are more likely to be adventitious colonists.

The most important point to note is that a clear majority of the thirteen principal species – those, that is, present in more than 10 per cent of Norfolk hedges – will, if properly managed, make a reasonable hedge. Hawthorn and blackthorn, as we have seen, were always the preferred hedging plant: both are easily propagated and bear formidable thorns. But early writers also recommended the use of holly, crab and hazel (Johnson 1978, 197–9; Fitzherbert 1534, 53; Norden 1609, 201; Cook 1676, 138). The first, with its sharp spines, makes an excellent barrier to stock as well as providing good winter fodder, while the others make a serviceable boundary hedge if plashed or coppiced and also provide fruit, and nuts, respectively (some early writers argued against their use on the grounds that they would attract trespassers!). Oak,* sycamore, elm and ash were widely recommended as hedgerow trees by

---

* Most Norfolk oaks are pendunculate, although sessile oak is found in some hedges in the north of the county.

FIGURE 26.
Hawthorn, the most
common species in
English hedges, and
always the favoured
hedging plant.

FIGURE 27.
Blackthorn or sloe has
sharp thorns and
propagates easily, but
its suckering habit can
produce wide,
spreading hedges in
pasture land.

sixteenth-, seventeenth- and eighteenth-century writers but the last two, in particular, will also make a good hedge in their own right. They both sprout vigorously, while elm has the bonus of being salt-resistant and thus eminently suitable for planting near the coast, as well as providing a good source of 'leafy hay'. Both species, moreover, but ash in particular, would provide excellent fuel wood when the hedge was plashed or coppiced, as also would maple. Indeed, of these thirteen most common hedge shrubs only three – dogwood, elder, and rose – would contribute little in terms of fuel or fruit, or provide a firm obstacle to stock, although rose (as we have seen) was sporadically used as a hedging plant.

Of course, the fact that the majority of the most common plants found in Norfolk hedges could have been intentionally planted there does not mean that they were. Hawthorn, blackthorn and ash are all rapid colonisers while maple, as we shall see, will arrive in a hedge much faster than some writers have assumed. Yet on the other hand, both hazel and oak are rather poor colonisers, while the majority of elm must certainly have been planted close to where it now grows. Most examples are of the narrow-leafed East Anglian variety *Ulmus carpinifolia*, dominant in Norfolk, Suffolk, north Essex and into the adjacent areas of Cambridgeshire and Hertfordshire (Richens 1983, 4–5; Rackham 1986, 234–6, 245): the small-leafed English elm, *Ulmus procera*, is rare here, and wych elm, *Ulmus glabra*, seems to have been only sporadically planted as a timber tree.* *Carpinifolia* no longer propagates easily from seed, but only by suckering, and while some of the examples recorded may

---

* The taxonomy of elms is complex, confusing, and debated. The main forms found in East Anglia are *Ulmus carpinifolia*, variously called 'East Anglian' or smooth-leaved elm, which may or may not be native and which does not usually set viable seed, reproducing mainly by suckering; *Ulmus Glabra*, or wych elm, the large-leaved variety which is certainly native and which will produce viable seed; and *U. procera*, English elm, sometimes classified as *U. minor* subsp. *minor*, which is not native and which does not produce seed.

well have suckered into the hedge from adjoining areas of woodland, most must presumably have been intentionally established there. Conversely, it is also noteworthy that very few of the rarer hedgerow plants (those present in less than 10 per cent of Norfolk hedges) were ever recommended by early writers, either for hedging or for timber: many (such as guelder rose, aspen, the two buckthorns, spindle) would contribute little to a hedge. In short, it is perfectly possible that many of the shrubs found in Norfolk hedges were, in fact, planted there, rather than being adventitious arrivals in what was originally a single-species hedge.

As already noted, methods of management – both contemporary and historical – can have a significant impact on the species content of hedges. It is often assumed that Norfolk has no strong tradition of laying or plashing, hedges here having always been managed by coppicing. This impression is largely due to eighteenth- and nineteenth-century writers, especially William Marshall. He described how, in the area of north-east Norfolk with which he was most familiar, plashing was entirely unknown. Hedges were instead managed by coppicing, largely because of the shortage of managed woodland in the district and the pressing need for firewood:

> Old hedges, in general, abound with oak, ash and maple stubs, off which the wood is cut every time the hedge is felled; also with pollards, whose heads are another source of firewood (Marshall 1787, 96).

The entire supply of wood and timber in the district, he added, 'may be said, with little latitude, to be from hedge-rows'. Both Marshall, and his contemporary Nathaniel Kent, also refer to the practice of *buckstalling*, where hedges were cut back, not to the base of the shrubs, but at a height of between two and three feet (*c.* 0.6 – 1 m), something of which they both disapproved as it tended to make the hedge bare out at the base (Kent 1796, 182). The only references to plashing made by eighteenth- and nineteenth-century Norfolk writers is as a method of dealing with neglected or decayed hedges. R. N. Bacon, writing in 1844, thus quoted with approval the comments of one Mr Withers, from Holt:

> Where hedges are properly formed and kept, they can seldom require to be plashed; but this mode of treating a hedge is most valuable in the cases of the fences abounding with hedge-row timber, when from neglect or any other cause the hedge has become of irregular growth (Bacon 1844, 390).

It is possible that the occasional signs of plashing exhibited by old hedges in their present growth pattern are simply evidence of such radical 'first aid' (Figure 28). But on the other hand, stray documentary references from before the eighteenth century suggest that management by regular plashing may once have been more usual in Norfolk. At Raynham in 1664 the steward gave instructions 'to plash the hedges behind the garden and that next the heath' (Saunders 1917) while in 1516 John Skayman, an earlier steward for the

Raynham estate, recorded how he 'was at Bermer to see who [how] the stakes and hogyn wood lay', ready for the hedgers there. The latter promised him that as soon as the weather improved they 'schuld be heggyn ther as fast as thei cane for they cane done no good now for by cause the frost is so grete that thei canne sette no stakes' (Moreton and Rutledge 1996, 121). The 'stakes' were presumably the upright poles or 'stabbers' through which the pleachers of a laid hedge were to be woven. Similarly, in 1472 payments were made for 'digging, plashing and hedging' the boundary of Sporle Wood (Gairdner 1896). Such references imply that plashing may well have been more common in Norfolk in medieval and early modern times than it was by the end of the eighteenth century, and its decline may have been due, at least in part, to the increasingly arable character of the local economy, and to a concomitant decline in the need for stock-proof fences, coupled with a rising population and an escalating need for fuel. Coppicing, as already noted, produces more firewood.

Conclusion

We have now examined the complex natural and historical context of Norfolk's hedges, and what little is known from documentary sources about their planting and management. The key points of this discussion are perhaps worth summarising briefly. First, although the county's soil regions, landscape regions and agricultural geography are highly complex a useful distinction can be made between areas of light, easily-leached soils, and the claylands. The former were denuded of woodland at an early date and were largely, although never entirely, devoid of hedges until the later seventeenth century. The latter, in contrast, remained relatively well-wooded into modern times and were already extensively hedged by the start of the seventeenth century. The light, leached lands were dominated by large estates; the clays were, for the most part, characterised by a plethora of small properties. The loam districts of the north-east can, for most purposes, be considered as lying between these two extremes. Second, an examination of the (admittedly sparse) documentary evidence, coupled with a consideration of the essential characteristics of the species most commonly found in Norfolk hedges, suggests that before *c.*1700 hedges may have been planted with a rather greater range of species than after this date; and that even in the eighteenth and nineteenth centuries more than one species might, on occasions, be planted in a hedge, even if only as timber. Lastly, we have suggested that while by the eighteenth century Norfolk hedges were universally managed by coppicing (or 'buckstalling'), in earlier centuries plashing may have been more widely practiced. With these basic parameters established, we can now turn to the field evidence for the origins and development of the county's varied hedges.

CHAPTER FOUR

Hedges: Composition, Age and Environment

....

The survey

The purpose of our research was not simply to evaluate how far the 'Hooper hypothesis' stands up to close scrutiny. It was also to gain a fuller understanding of all the factors – natural as well as human – leading to diversity in the character of hedges, and to explore other ways in which the composition of hedges might throw light on the wider history of the landscape. Norfolk, as we have seen, is a particularly good area in which to undertake such an endeavour because of its considerable range of soil types, and of land use and enclosure histories. Initially a number of volunteers were asked to record the hedges in their own parishes. A small number of these surveys were, in the event, disregarded as unreliable, and further surveys of selected parishes were undertaken by the authors, assisted by Sarah Harrison; and by Patsy Dallas, Lucy Whittle and Anne Wood. Over a number of years from 1996 to 2004 we thus built up a database of some 2,800 hedges, from 120 parishes in the county, the number surveyed in each parish ranging from a minimum of 7 to a maximum of 271. The hedges were all recorded on standard forms, in thirty-metre sections, with a minimum of three sections being recorded for each hedge. The sample was spread across all the soil types and landscape regions discussed in the previous chapter (Figure 29). Some discussion of the initial survey results has already been presented (Barnes, Parmenter and Williamson 1998). But many of the suggestions then made did not stand the test of time, as the survey work continued and as more data was accumulated.

FIGURE 29.
The Norfolk hedge and boundary survey: the distribution of sample parishes.

Given the scope of the survey and the numbers of people involved it is inevitable that certain aspects were recorded in more detail or with greater consistency than others. For example, it is possible that bullace is under-represented in the sample due to confusion with the ubiquitous blackthorn; the same is true to an even greater degree of marabellum, cherry plum, and other members of the *Prunus* genus. Such problems are, as we shall see, especially serious with regard to the recording of 'woodland relic' herbs, which was certainly inconsistent. Nevertheless, the sheer size of the body of data collected, combined with the particular ways in which we have analysed and interrogated it, give some confidence in the results here presented.

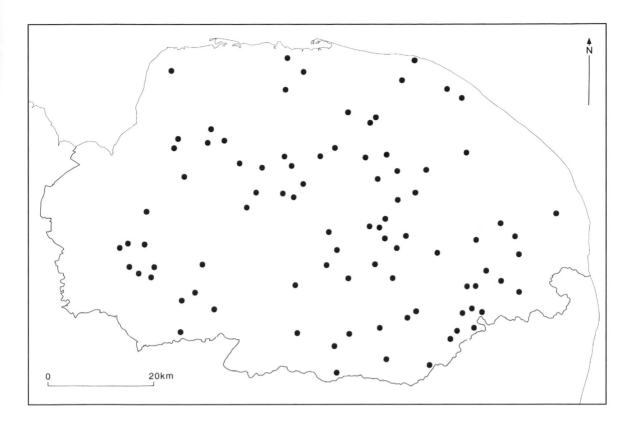

The analysis

The ideal method of analysing the information would have been to enter into a database the principal characteristics of each thirty-metre sample length of hedge, but this would have been a massive and repetitive task. The 2,800 hedges recorded totalled, in all, over 15,000 separate samples, and for each of these a number of different variables relating to species content, character of ground flora, and various topographic and historical information would need to be entered. Instead, a simpler method was adopted: each hedge was treated as an entity and its overall characteristics analysed. There are obvious problems with such a procedure. Firstly, in so far as species content is related to environmental and locational factors, such as soil type or proximity to woodland, changes in these over the length of a hedge – when it extends across a junction of soil types, for example, from heavy clay to acid sand, or where one end buts up against an area of woodland – might change the hedge significantly and, when averaging out compositional character along its entire length, obscure the clarity of any relationship with such factors. Secondly, sections of hedge might have been subjected to complete replanting at some stage in the past. Thirdly, and most importantly, what might today appear as a single 'hedge' can often appear on earlier maps as a number of separate hedges, forming the boundary between several contiguous fields. Its present appearance as a unitary feature, in other words, is the consequence of later rationalisation and boundary removal. A related problem concerns hedges following roads or parish boundaries. It is easy to assume that these will be of the same date throughout their length, but this is not necessarily so. A road running through an area of unhedged open field, for example, might have become hedged in sections as the surrounding fields were enclosed, piecemeal, in a series of stages. While the road itself might be all of one date, the hedges bounding it would not be. Similarly, we know that many parish boundaries originally ran in part through areas of open common land and 'waste' on the margins of agricultural territories. As, in the course of the medieval and post-medieval periods, these areas were assarted and encroached upon, and finally enclosed, a line originally notional – from one feature (pond, tree) to another – or else marked by a minor ditch, would become a continuous hedge line. Again, while the boundary itself might have been decided at a single point in time the hedge that follows it could be an amalgam of ages.

Some measures can be taken to limit the effects of these problems. In particular, where a single 'hedge' displays a marked change in character, and where this coincides with a change in direction, a minor kink, or other feature suggesting a break in continuity, then it was analysed as two or more separate hedges. The same procedure was followed where noticeable alterations in the character of hedges on roadsides or parish boundaries coincided with changes in direction, or with points where major boundaries butted up against them. It goes without saying that such complexities of boundary history are not always observable, and that in some cases two or more hedges with very differing origins will have been treated as one in the following analysis. Nevertheless, once again the sheer size of the sample studied here ought to be enough to limit the overall impact of such factors on any observed patterning in the data.

Further problems arise from the fact that the data, as already noted, was collected by different researchers, at different times of the year, so that not all results are closely comparable. In particular, while some surveys recorded significant ground flora – principally, the supposed 'woodland relic herbs' – systematically, with others coverage was less complete or reliable: either because of the abilities of the surveyor or, more usually, because surveys were carried out in the summer when much of this significant vegetation is obscured by the growth of common grasses, nettles, umbellifers and other plants. Again, it was possible to note all those hedge lengths in which a nil response regarding the presence or absence of such plants was likely to be unreliable, still leaving a considerable body of data which could be meaningfully analysed. Similar problems concern observations relating to the extent to which the hedge was dominated by a particular species (such as hawthorn) or was thoroughly 'mixed' in character – these characteristics were not recorded by all surveyors, and are anyway to some extent a matter of subjective observation. But once again the information was used when recorded, and a nil response was not equated with a negative record.

With these problems and caveats in mind we can turn to the actual methods used to analyse the data. A relatively simple database was constructed in which – in addition to an identifying number – the characteristics of each hedge were entered under a number of fields. The various species present were listed in full, and the average number per thirty-metre length was calculated. If a species, or more than one, appeared dominant this was recorded; if the observer considered the hedge to be thoroughly mixed and without a clear dominant, this was duly noted. The next field was more complex. Both an initial analysis of our results, and the surveys carried out in other areas of England described in the previous chapter, suggested a broad distinction between, on the one hand, those trees and shrubs found in most hedges, and those present only in hedges of known or suspected antiquity and, conversely, rare in hedges known to have been planted during the last two or three centuries. The latter can further be divided between those – like hornbeam – present only in a relatively small proportion of hedges, and those which are fairly common – hazel, dogwood, and maple. This field therefore simply recorded, for each hedge, whether at least two of these species were present in a majority of the sample lengths.

The presence of significant ground flora was noted – the 'woodland relic' herbs such as dog's mercury, bluebell, wood anemone, or primrose; and the hedge was classified in terms of the character or form of the boundary with which it was associated. This was done under a number of headings: roadsides, parish boundaries, present or former common boundaries, boundaries evidently resulting from piecemeal enclosure of open fields, boundaries created by parliamentary enclosure or similar relatively recent planned reorganisations of the landscape, and 'irregular' boundaries. A hedge could have one or more of these attributes; it could, for example, be associated with an irregular road which also formed a parish boundary.

In another field we noted, where known, the dates within which a hedge apparently came into existence, usually on the basis of its non-appearance on a map of known date and its appearance on another. This information was coded into fifty-year periods from 'before 1600' (A) to '1850–1900' ('G') so that, for example, a hedge absent from a map of 1627 but present on one of 1750 would be coded 'BCD'. Absolute dates of planting were also given and appropriately coded, where known (i.e., with a single letter – 'B', 'F', etc.). A further field gave the soil association on which the hedge was growing, taken from the maps published by the Soil Survey of England and Wales (Hodge *et al.* 1984).

Species number and age

A total of 61 different shrub species were recorded in Norfolk hedges by the survey, although with widely differing frequencies. At one extreme, hawthorn was present in nearly all (around 97 per cent) of the hedges. At the other, wild service was recorded in a mere five. More importantly, as in other parts of the country, individual hedges displayed a considerable degree of variation in

shrub content, with some dominated by hawthorn and with few other species,
while others were more mixed in character and contained large numbers of
different shrubs. The first issue which we shall address is the extent to which
such variations are primarily related to the age of hedges, as Hooper and others
have argued.

As already noted, we can attribute broad or actual planting dates to some
hedges by using maps and documents, although this applies to fewer hedges
than originally anticipated, owing in part to ambiguities in the cartographic
evidence. Just over fifty of the hedges examined in the survey can be dated
with confidence to the period before *c.*1600 and these are, for the most part,
very mixed in character, with an average of 5.6 species per thirty metres of
length. Hawthorn is the most frequent species, but only just: rose, ash, blackthorn, oak, elm, elder, maple, hazel and dogwood are all present in more than
half of the recorded hedges. Those examples known to have been planted
between *c.*1600 and 1750 – slightly fewer in number – are surprisingly similar
in character: well-mixed, and with an average of five species in each thirty-
metre length. Again, hawthorn is only just the most common species. Rose,
ash, blackthorn, elder, oak, elm, maple, and hazel are again each present in
over half the hedges: indeed, the only noticeable difference between the two
groups is the slightly lower frequency of dogwood in these later hedges.

Hedges known to have been planted after 1750 – a very much larger group
– are very different in character. They have an average of only 3 shrub species
per thirty metres of length. Hawthorn is by far their most important component: only ash, rose, blackthorn, elder and oak are present in more than half
the hedges, with most of the latter in the form of standard trees. While maple
is again moderately common, hazel and dogwood are rare.

The number of dated hedges in the two older groups is very small but
their similarity, and the extent to which they differ from the post-1750
hedges, is striking: hedges planted in the seventeenth and early eighteenth
century appear far closer in character to those planted before *c.*1600 than
to those established after 1750. This observation mirrors that made by
Willmott regarding hedges in Church Broughton: that examples first shown
on maps of 1630, and of 1775, contained almost identical numbers of species;
or the conclusions reached by Hall regarding Yorkshire hedges, that those
planted at any time before the eighteenth century tended to form a 'statistically indistinguishable group' (above, page 35: Willmott 1980, 282–4; Hall
1982, 102–5). However – and again to some extent echoing the findings of
Willmott and Hall – for hedges planted after the mid-eighteenth century
there *does* seem to be a correlation between species number and age. Those
known to have originated between 1750 and 1800 thus have 3.9 species per
thirty metres; those planted between 1800 and 1850, – 187 examples – have
an average of 3; while the very small number planted after 1850 – nine in all
– have an average of only 1.9.

Hedges even broadly dated by documentary or cartographic evidence, especially from the period before *c.*1750, constitute only a minority of the sample

and the observed contrast – between relatively recent hedges dominated by hawthorn, and which display some correlation between age and species number; and earlier hedges which tend to form a single, statistically indivisible group – should be treated with some caution. There is, however, another way in which we can break down the sample hedges into broad age-ranges: by considering the morphology of the boundaries with which they are associated. In general terms we can assume that the overwhelming majority of boundaries which are ruler-straight in character are of post-1700 age, while those resulting from the piecemeal enclosure of open fields are on the whole earlier, with the majority of examples dating to the period *c.* 1450–1750. Those of 'irregular' form, especially those growing on roads, former common edges or on parish and hundred boundaries, are likely to include the oldest hedges in Norfolk, although a number of examples will be considerably younger than the boundaries which they now follow, as for example where a road running through open fields became hedged only in the course of the post-medieval period. The vast majority of hedges in the sample can be placed into one or other of these three groups, and when analysed the data can, with some confidence, be discussed in statistical terms, and displayed graphically (Figure 30).

It is immediately apparent that, once again, the hedges in the two 'older' categories – those of 'irregular' form, and those created by piecemeal enclosure – are very similar in character. In both, hawthorn is the dominant species but a large number of other shrubs are abundant, and are present in more than half the recorded hedges: rose, ash, blackthorn, elder, oak, elm, maple and hazel. Dogwood, while less frequent, is nevertheless common, although more so in the 'irregular' hedges. Both types of hedge have an average of 4.6 species per thirty metres, and more or less the same proportion of each was considered to be 'mixed' (that is, without a clearly dominant species) by recorders – 40 per cent and 38 per cent respectively. In addition, at least two of the three most important 'slow colonisers' – hazel, maple and dogwood – were present in a majority of sample lengths in roughly the same proportion of hedges of 'irregular' and 'piecemeal enclosure' type – 18 per cent and 19 per cent respectively.

Yet while these two categories of hedge seem barely, if at all, distinguishable, they both contrast markedly with those in the 'straight' category, mostly of post-1700 origin. These have, on average, only 3.7 species per thirty metres and are mainly dominated by hawthorn, or (more rarely) by a mixture of hawthorn and blackthorn. Only 19 per cent were considered 'mixed' by recorders, and at least two of the key 'slow colonisers' (maple, dogwood, hazel) were present together in a majority of sample lengths in a mere 2.3 per cent of examples. Only rose, elder, hawthorn and blackthorn were present in more than 50 per cent of the hedges; ash, elm and oak were moderately common, and crab and maple were recorded in around a quarter; but hazel and dogwood were both rare.

What is striking about these results is not so much the close similarity displayed by the 'irregular' and 'piecemeal enclosure' hedges, for the former

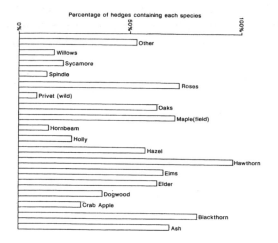

Percentage of hedges containing each species

Other
Willows
Sycamore
Spindle
Roses
Privet (wild)
Oaks
Maple(field)
Hornbeam
Holly
Hazel
Hawthorn
Elms
Elder
Dogwood
Crab Apple
Blackthorn
Ash

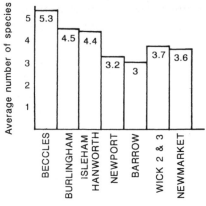

A: HEDGES OF "IRREGULAR" TYPE

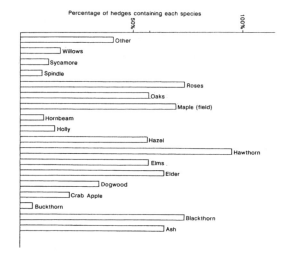

Percentage of hedges containing each species

Other
Willows
Sycamore
Spindle
Roses
Oaks
Maple (field)
Hornbeam
Holly
Hazel
Hawthorn
Elms
Elder
Dogwood
Crab Apple
Buckthorn
Blackthorn
Ash

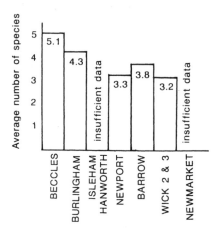

B: HEDGES CREATED BY PIECEMEAL ENCLOSURE

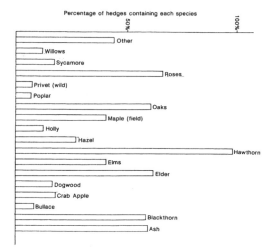

Percentage of hedges containing each species

Other
Willows
Sycamore
Roses
Privet (wild)
Poplar
Oaks
Maple (field)
Holly
Hazel
Hawthorn
Elms
Elder
Dogwood
Crab Apple
Bullace
Blackthorn
Ash

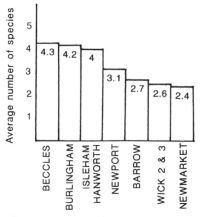

C: HEDGES OF "STRAIGHT", EIGHTEENTH AND NINETEENTH-CENTURY TYPE

are a diverse group which, while including many medieval hedges, will also contain some of comparatively recent origin: but rather the great difference between the hedges in the 'piecemeal enclosure' and the 'straight' groups. Almost all of the former, as noted, must have been planted between *c.*1450 and 1750; the latter mainly originated between *c.*1700 and 1830. Most of the hedges in these two groups must have been planted within two and half centuries, *c.*1550–1800, and yet the character of each differs more radically than we might expect, if age were the sole or main determinant of diversity. This clearly mirrors the pattern displayed by the much smaller sample of 'dated' hedges, already discussed. It is, perhaps, worth noting that almost all of the difference in average species number between the two groups is accounted for by the much greater frequency in the piecemeal enclosure hedges of three species, elm, maple and hazel, all of which might well have been intentionally planted, in early times, as part of a hedge.

Taken together, this evidence suggests that most hedges established before the eighteenth century were planted with varying mixtures of two or more species, rather than with hawthorn or blackthorn alone. While new 'colonists' might, as Hooper's hypothesis suggests, have subsequently arrived at a relatively constant rate, these would constitute additions to hedges of unknown original composition and, in consequence, for pre-eighteenth century hedges at least, there could be no meaningful relationship between species content and age. It is hardly surprising, then, that such hedges appear to coalesce into a single 'statistically indistinguishable group'.

But *were* rates of colonisation relatively constant across time and space? In fact, the Norfolk data suggests that they were not. One indication of this is the way that, in general terms, variations in the average number of species found in hedges are closely related to soil type. On average, hedges growing on clay soils, and on damp peats, boast a greater number of species than those on the more leached and droughty soils. The 909 hedges recorded on the heavy clays of the Beccles 3 association thus have an average of 5 species per 30 metres; the 520 on the slightly lighter clays of the Burlingham 1 and 3 associations, 4.3; while the 119 recorded on the damp peats of the Isleham and Hanworth associations have 4.1. The 417 hedges growing on the well-drained loams of the Wick 2 and 3 associations have 3.4, and the 88 on the acid sands of the Newport 4 association have 3.2. The 117 on the dry sandy soils of the Barrow association have an average of 3, while the 281 on the chalky soils of the Newmarket 2 and 3 associations boast a mere 2.7.* Across Norfolk, the extent of variation associated with soil type, ranging from 2.7 to 5 species per thirty metres of hedge, is in fact significantly greater than that which we can attribute to age on any *single* soil type. Of course, these average figures are

FIGURE 30.
opposite left
The frequency of the
principal shrub species
in the three main forms
of Norfolk hedge.
Top: those of
'irregular' form.
Middle: those created
by piecemeal enclosure.
Bottom: those growing
on straight boundaries
of eighteenth- and
nineteenth-century
date. (Only those
species present in more
than 5 per cent of
hedges are shown
separately).

FIGURE 31.
opposite right
The average number of
species per thirty
metres of hedge length
found in the three
main types of hedge,
by soil type.

---

* The numbers of hedges recorded on the various other soil types represented in the county (such as the Hanslope association, the Ollerton association, the Worlington association and the Methwold association) were too few in number to be treated in a statistical manner, although they are mentioned at various points in the discussions that follow.

distorted by the fact that some soils were, in general, enclosed earlier than others, and therefore simply have a higher proportion of old hedges. It is striking, then, that the same pattern emerges when we compare the species content of *boundaries of similar age on different types of soil.* This is most easily done by examining the 'straight' boundaries which, with few exceptions, were planted in the period after *c.*1700, and mainly between 1750 and 1850. On the heavy clay soils of the Beccles 3 association such relatively young boundaries have an average of 4.3 species per 30 metres, those on the slightly lighter Burlingham soils have 4.2 and those on the Isleham/Hanworth soils 4. Examples growing on the acid sands of the Newport 4 association, in contrast, have 3.1, those on the Barrow association, 2.7, those on the Wick associations 2.6 and those on the Newmarket soils, 2.4. The same broad 'gradient' of values is displayed by hedges of 'irregular' character, and those created by piecemeal enclosure (Figure 31), the former ranging from 5.3 on the Beccles soils to 3 on those of the Barrow soils, the latter from 5.1 on Beccles soils to 3.2 on the Wick soils. The *precise* pattern is not mirrored, it is true, by these different hedge types, but the overall trend is clear enough. Hedges of similar dates and origins generally have more species on clay soils, and on damp peats, than on the drier loams and sands.

There are two possible explanations for this relationship. Firstly, woodland survived better on the clays and peats than on the lighter lands, and hedges were more prominent on these soils from an early date, thus ensuring a greater abundance of seed sources than were present in the lighter 'champion' lands. Secondly, the more fertile and moisture-retentive character of these soils ensured higher rates of colonisation than drier and often more acid conditions. In addition, it is possible that on the clays even hedges established in the eighteenth and nineteenth centuries were, on average, planted with a greater number of species than those on the lighter soils, because there were more small proprietors here who – to save money, or because of the ways in which they were using and managing their hedges – chose to plant them with a number of species, rather than with hawthorn alone.

The available evidence does not allow us to distinguish easily between these possibilities. In particular, the survey did not systematically analyse the effects on species content of proximity to woodland, in part because this has changed considerably in detail over the centuries, and in part because 'colonists' are as likely to derive from neighbouring hedges as from woods. Nevertheless, the survey results are enough to suggest that, while such *indirect* effects might be important, the *direct* influence of soil character accounts for much of the observed variation. On all soils the relatively recent 'straight' hedges are dominated by the same plants, either rapid colonisers or timber species: hawthorn, ash, blackthorn, elder, rose, elm, and oak. Much of the variation in average species number exhibited by such hedges on different soil types is due to an increased representation of one or more of these species, rather than to the abundance of other kinds of shrub. In particular, in hedges growing on clay soils, and on damp peats, both blackthorn and ash are much more frequent than in hedges found on the lighter loams and sands (Figure 32). As both species are widely distributed in the landscape, in woods, hedges and scrub, their better representation in these hedges suggests that they are able to establish themselves more quickly and more successfully there. Many previous studies have suggested that, while variations in soils may affect the particular *varieties* of species found in hedges, they will have no significant effect on the *numbers* of species present (Hewlett 1974, 95–6). The results of the Norfolk survey suggest that this assertion is wrong.

Yet the *indirect* effects of soil variation – differences in seed supply, and possibly in the original character of planting – may also have had an effect on colonisation rates. Although not the primary explanation for the differences in average species numbers exhibited by hedges growing on different soils, it is nevertheless true that the slow-colonising 'woodland' species, as identified by Hooper and Pollard (maple, hazel and dogwood) are more prominent in 'straight' hedges on the clays than in those found in other contexts. This is especially the case with maple, the fourth most commonly recorded plant in these recent hedges on the Beccles 3 association soils, but present in less than a fifth of those on lighter land (Figure 32). Moreover, while hazel and dogwood are both found in around a third of the 'straight' clayland hedges they are present at only very low frequencies, or are absent altogether, from hedges on drier soils, whether calcareous or acidic in character. These differences must be largely due to the fact that sufficient woods and hedges always existed on the clays to provide a substantial reservoir of seeds available for colonisation, and a source of seedlings for planting new hedges. The peaty Isleham and Hanworth soils, as we might expect given their widespread distribution in river valleys throughout the county, fall somewhere between the clays and the lighter soils in the proportions of these woodland shrubs which they contain.

As Hooper himself acknowledged, there are thus considerable variations in the rate at which hedges in different areas acquire new shrub species, variations which appear to be related to soil type both directly – in that they result from differences in fertility and moisture content – and indirectly – in that they are a consequence of variations in seed supply and, perhaps, the agrarian, and therefore social and tenurial, characteristics of the districts in question. This, coupled with the fact that many early hedges were originally planted with a range of species, presumably explains another pattern which is noticeable in the data, the tendency for the differences in species content between older and newer hedges to be more muted in some districts than in others. This is most easily demonstrated using detailed case studies from two areas with very different soils and landscapes, but which both have an abundance of maps, allowing the majority of their hedges to be at least broadly dated.

The Houghton estate in north-west Norfolk – which extends across the parishes of Harpley, West Rudham, and Houghton itself – was systematically mapped in 1720, at which time much of its area still lay in unenclosed sheepwalks and open fields. By 1836, when another survey was prepared, most open land had disappeared except Harpley Common, abutting on the Roman road Peddar's Way in the far west of Harpley parish (Houghton Hall archives, map 1 (Thomas Badeslade 1720), map 21 (Jonathan Hill 1836)). By 1886, when the Ordnance Survey First Edition six inch map was surveyed, not only had Harpley Common been enclosed but a number of alterations had been made to the existing field pattern, involving the amalgamation of fields and/or the straightening of boundaries created by earlier piecemeal enclosure. The soils across this area are fairly uniform: dry, slightly acid sands of the Barrow association, interspersed here and there with patches of clayey drift, and with some limited areas of more calcareous Newmarket 2 association soils. Ninety-eight hedges on the estate were recorded. Those associated with boundaries that were already in existence in 1720 – some perhaps with medieval origins, others probably the consequence of sixteenth- and seventeenth-century piecemeal enclosure – have, on average, 4.3 species per thirty metres; those created during the next 116 years have 3. Hedges planted since 1836, however, have on average slightly fewer, 2.7.

The parish of Morley lies on the clay plateau of central Norfolk and was mapped in 1624 by the surveyor Thomas Waterman (NRO PD3/108(H)). At this time the land consisted of hedged lanes and hedged fields – most of the latter, to judge from their outline, the consequence of piecemeal enclosure – interspersed with areas of open field, woods, and common land. By 1815 the open fields had been removed by piecemeal enclosure but the commons remained (NRO PD 3/109 CL). These were enclosed by a parliamentary act in that year: the enclosure award is accompanied by a map which shows the pattern of boundaries within the parish as a whole – i.e., both the 'old' and the 'new' enclosures. Subsequent minor changes to the boundary pattern are recorded on further maps, from 1840 (the Tithe Award: NRO 623) and 1881 (the Ordnance Survey First Edition six inch). Fifty-three hedges were surveyed in the parish, mainly on the experimental farm managed by the Norfolk Agricultural Research Station (now the Arable Group), in an area dominated by soils of the Burlingham 1 association but with extensive areas of Beccles 3 association soils. Hedges associated with boundaries already shown on the 1624 map have an average of 5.9 species per thirty metres; those which came into existence between 1624 and 1815, in contrast, have 4.6; while those created by the enclosure of the commons in 1815, and by the various minor changes to the boundary pattern which occurred in the course of the nineteenth century, have 4.8. In other words, the hedges growing on the moist and fertile clays of Morley display noticeably less age-related variation – or, to put it another way, have species-counts which are more 'bunched' in character – than those found on the light, acid lands of the Houghton estate.

These differences also appear to some extent when we consider the entire sample of hedges in the county in terms of the three broad chronological groups of hedges already discussed: those growing on straight boundaries; those associated with boundaries created by early piecemeal enclosures; and

FIGURE 32.
The frequency of the principal shrub species in hedges growing on straight boundaries of eighteenth- and nineteenth-century date, by soil type (only those species present in more than 5 per cent of hedges are shown separately).

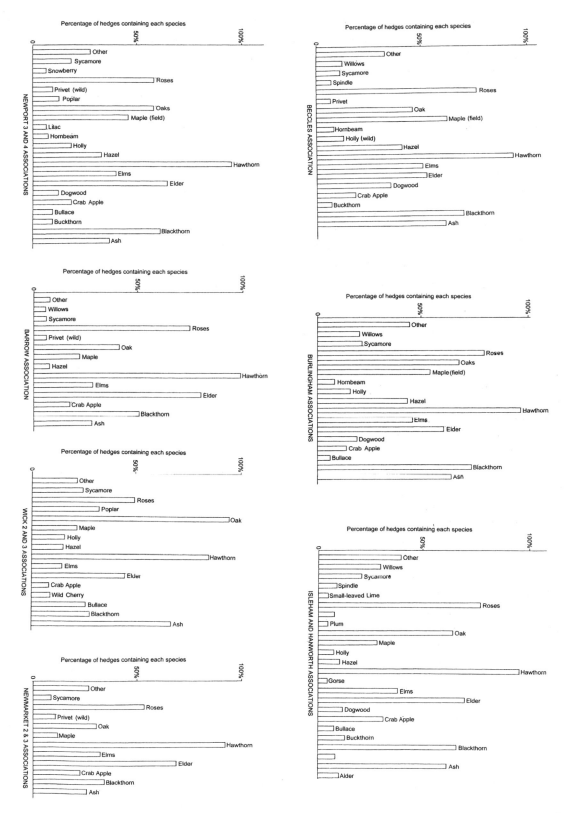

Percentage of hedges containing each species

NEWPORT 3 AND 4 ASSOCIATIONS

Other
Sycamore
Snowberry
Roses
Privet (wild)
Poplar
Oaks
Maple (field)
Lilac
Hornbeam
Holly
Hazel
Hawthorn
Elms
Elder
Dogwood
Crab Apple
Bullace
Buckthorn
Blackthorn
Ash

Percentage of hedges containing each species

BECCLES ASSOCIATION

Other
Willows
Sycamore
Spindle
Roses
Privet
Oak
Maple (field)
Hornbeam
Holly (wild)
Hazel
Hawthorn
Elms
Elder
Dogwood
Crab Apple
Buckthorn
Blackthorn
Ash

Percentage of hedges containing each species

BARROW ASSOCIATION

Other
Willows
Sycamore
Roses
Privet (wild)
Oak
Maple
Hazel
Hawthorn
Elms
Elder
Crab Apple
Blackthorn
Ash

Percentage of hedges containing each species

BURLINGHAM ASSOCIATIONS

Other
Willows
Sycamore
Roses
Oaks
Maple (field)
Hornbeam
Holly
Hazel
Hawthorn
Elms
Elder
Dogwood
Crab Apple
Bullace
Blackthorn
Ash

Percentage of hedges containing each species

WICK 2 AND 3 ASSOCIATIONS

Other
Sycamore
Roses
Poplar
Oak
Maple
Holly
Hazel
Hawthorn
Elms
Elder
Crab Apple
Wild Cherry
Bullace
Blackthorn
Ash

Percentage of hedges containing each species

ISLEHAM AND HANWORTH ASSOCIATIONS

Other
Willows
Sycamore
Spindle
Small-leaved Lime
Roses
Plum
Oak
Maple
Holly
Hazel
Hawthorn
Gorse
Elms
Elder
Dogwood
Crab Apple
Bullace
Buckthorn
Blackthorn
Ash
Alder

Percentage of hedges containing each species

NEWMARKET 2 & 3 ASSOCIATIONS

Other
Sycamore
Roses
Privet (wild)
Oak
Maple
Hawthorn
Elms
Elder
Crab Apple
Blackthorn
Ash

those growing on 'irregular' boundaries. The 'irregular' hedges growing on the light, porous soils of the Newmarket 2 association have an average of 3.6 species per thirty metres, while those in the 'straight' category have 2.4.* 'Irregular' hedges on Beccles 3 soils in contrast have 5.3 species per thirty metres, 'piecemeal enclosure' hedges have 5.1, and 'straight' hedges 4.3; while on Burlingham association soils the figures are 4.5, 4.3 and 4.2. Variations in species content due to age, it would seem, are most muted in areas where traditions of mixed-species planting were strong, because of environmental and tenurial circumstances; and where an abundance of woods and hedges provided a ready source of new colonisers.

One other factor appears to have had some importance in generating variation in the species content of Norfolk's hedges. Both Fowler and Willmott noted in their studies how roadside hedges are, in general, more species-rich than field hedges, and to a slight extent this also appears to be true of Norfolk (Fowler 1974, 37–8; Willmott 1980, 280–81). Across the county as a whole roadside hedges thus have an average of 4.2 species per thirty-metre section, while field hedges have only 3.9. This pattern is repeated across all soil types, although on average the difference is greater on soils of the Newmarket association than on others, and is virtually non-existent on Beccles 3 association soils. To an extent, this pattern may reflect that fact that in some areas roadside hedges are in reality generally older than field hedges, due to the particular way in which enclosure occurred. But what is striking is that the same pattern is repeated when we consider only road hedges and field hedges of eighteenth- and nineteenth-century date – those growing on 'straight' boundaries. Across all soil types, the average number of species in 'straight road' hedges is 3.7, against 3.2 for 'straight field' hedges (Figure 33). In this case, when the pattern is broken down by soil type the extent of the difference seems to be broadly related to the moisture-retention properties of the soils in question, so that the difference between the average number of species growing on 'straight road' and 'straight field' hedges is, on all the clayey and peaty soils, 0.3 species per thirty metres or less, while the lighter soils all have a difference greater than this. These figures suggest that while to some extent the difference between roadside and other hedges may be related to age, to a rather greater extent it reflects the fact that shrub species tend to establish themselves with slightly greater rapidity along roadsides, especially on those drier soils on which colonisation rates are in general lower. This may be because roadsides constitute relatively disturbed environments, due to the passage of traffic and animals. Alternatively, or in addition, they may function as channels for dispersal, seeds being moved along them by road-users. Willmott's observation that, in Church Broughton, the difference between roadside and field hedges was due to the greater numbers of timber trees planted in the former does not appear to be reflected in the Norfolk data.

* There are very few hedges on these soils which were created by piecemeal enclosure.

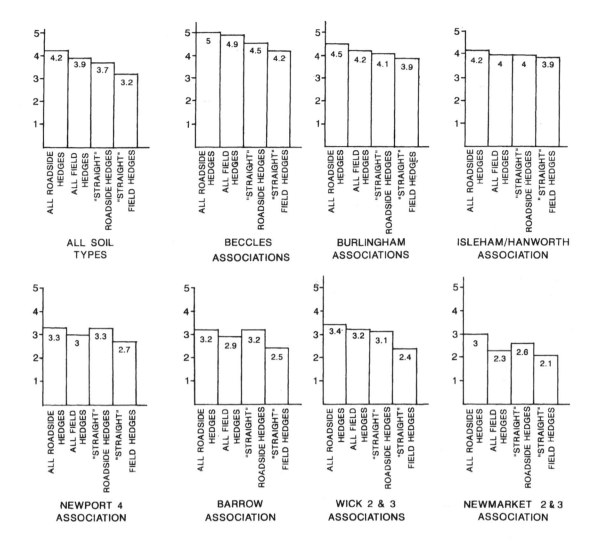

It might be helpful at this point to summarise briefly the preceding, some-what densely-argued pages. Careful analysis of this substantial body of data clearly suggests that there is a relationship between the age and species content of Norfolk hedges. Older hedges are in general more diverse in composition than younger ones. But the kind of simple, linear relationship between age and diversity sometimes postulated is only evident, and even then fairly weakly, on the lighter soils, and in the case of hedges planted since *c.* 1700. Pre-eighteenth-century hedges tend to be more uniform in character, and the survey results suggest that this is because they were normally planted with a greater range of species than more recent examples. Multi-species planting may have been particularly prevalent (and perhaps persisted longest) on the claylands, in part because this was an area in which small proprietors (rather than great estates) were important, in part because an abundance of woodland and pre-existing hedges provided a ready source of hedging plants. Natural colonisation rates were also higher here, because of the greater number of potential seed sources. But soil type has also had an important *direct* influence on the species content of hedges, in terms of soil moisture content and perhaps fertility. Indeed, across the county as a whole such natural factors are probably a greater influence on the composition and diversity of hedges than antiquity *per se*. Lastly, there is some evidence that roadside hedges have acquired new species at a slightly faster rate than those bordering fields, especially on the lighter soils. For all these reasons, it appears on first inspection unlikely that the floristic characteristics of any individual hedge can, in reality, tell us very much about its age.

Woodland relic hedges

As we saw in Chapter Two, Hooper and Pollard proposed not one but two explanations for species-rich hedges. Some originated through the colonisation, over a very long period of time, of hedges which had originally been planted with only one or two species. Others were of 'woodland relic' type: that is, they had been formed during assarting by medieval colonists who managed the existing woodland under-storey, by plashing, to form stock-proof barriers around their enclosures (Pollard 1973, 351; Pollard *et al.* 1974, 87). In terms of their shrub component, woodland relic hedges were characterised by their very mixed character, and by an abundance of such slowly colonising, characteristically woodland species as maple, hazel, dogwood, and woodland hawthorn (*Crataegus oxycanthoides*). Others have emphasised the significance of small-leafed lime or pry (*Tilia cordata*) and wild service tree (*Sorbus torminalis*) (Figure 34) in this respect. These are particularly powerful 'indicators' of woodland-assart origins because they do not, in present conditions, usually set seed, but regenerate only by suckering from the rootstock (Rackham 1986, 183, 203). In addition, woodland relic hedges have a distinctive herb layer, including bluebell, primrose, wood anemone, wood spurge, wood melick, yellow archangel, and dog's mercury (Figures 35 and 36). A further 20 species with strong woodland associations have been suggested by Helliwell, including wood avens (*Geum urbanum*) and barren strawberry (*Potentilla sterilis*): these were rare or absent from the more recent 'planted' hedges recorded in his survey and, he suggested, 'do not spread readily throughout the hedgerow network' (Helliwell 1975, 71).

How far does the Norfolk evidence support the idea of a distinct class of 'woodland relic' hedge? We may start by observing that the survey data, coupled with other information – most notably, the survey of Norfolk flora carried out by Gillian Beckett, Alec Bull, and Robin Stevenson in the 1990s – suggests that many of the additional herb species discussed by Helliwell are not, in fact, particularly restricted in their distribution (Beckett, Bull and Stevenson 1999). Wood avens, barren strawberry, bugle, betony, and most of the others can be found in hedges of all ages and origins in the county, and indeed in other non-woodland contexts. Wood avens, for example, was recorded in almost every sample grid square in Norfolk examined by Beckett and her colleagues, who concluded that it was 'widespread in shady places, quick to colonise new plantations' (Beckett, Bull and Stevenson 1999, 127). Not surprisingly, our own survey revealed that it was common even in parliamentary enclosure hedges. With the 'core' list of herbs originally proposed by Pollard – bluebell, primrose, wood anemone, wood spurge, wood melick, yellow archangel, and dog's mercury – the situation is more complex. Some of these species are so rare generally in Norfolk that they are of little use as indicators of particular types of hedge. Wood spurge, for example, was recorded in only a handful of hedges – all, it is true, of presumed antiquity, such as the parish boundary between Needham and Brockdish – and similarly appears in only 3 per cent of the sample squares recorded in Beckett's survey. Wood melick is also a relative rarity in Norfolk hedges, as are yellow archangel and wood anemone. On the heavy clays in the north of the parish of Wymondham, for example, where dog's mercury and primrose are widespread in hedges, wood anemone and yellow archangel were each recorded only twice (Figure 37).

Dog's mercury, bluebell and primrose are thus the most commonly recorded of Pollard's 'woodland relic' herbs in Norfolk; and of these, as in Pollard and Hooper's study, dog's mercury was by far the most frequently noted. In part this is because it is easily recognised not only in the spring but also during the summer months, growing in great masses and with a distinctive hue (Figure 35). But in part it is simply because it is the most common by far of these herbs. Its distribution is particularly interesting: it is most common in hedges growing on the heavier clay soils of the Beccles 3 association (69 per cent of records), and is more sparsely recorded in those on the lighter, more acid clays of the Burlingham 1 and 3 associations (18 per cent of records) and the heavy, more calcareous clays of the Hanslope association (8 per cent of records). In contrast, it is generally rare or absent on other soils (Figure 38), the only significant exception being the moist peat soils of the Isleham and Hanworth associations (3 per cent of records). Primrose mirrors this distribution fairly closely; but bluebell is less well represented on the boulder clays, being completely absent from the Hanslope soils – presumably because it prefers a neutral to acid, rather than alkaline, environment. It is correspondingly more prominent on some of the moderately acid soils away from the clays, especially those of the Wick 2 and 3 associations in the north-east of the county (Figure 38).

These distributions correspond, in general terms, with those areas in which large amounts of woodland existed at the time of Domesday, and in which hedges appear to have been moderately common from an early date, observations which are in line with the distribution of hedges containing woodland relic herbs noted by Hooper and Pollard in Huntingdonshire (Pollard *et al.* 1974, 90–1). But we need to examine the extent to which the correlation is *really* with woodland and early enclosure, rather than more directly with soil type. Is the absence of most of these herbs from the lighter soils, in other

FIGURE 34.
Wild service tree
(*Sorbus torminalis*) no
longer sets seed easily
and is thus a classic
indicator of a
'woodland relic' hedge.

FIGURE 35.
Dog's mercury
(*Mercurialis perennis*)
growing at the base of
a roadside hedge in
Morley in central
Norfolk. The plant is
particularly visible in
early spring, before it is
obscured by other
vegetation.

FIGURE 36.
Primrose (*Primula vulgaris*), growing in a hedge in Needham in south Norfolk.

FIGURE 37.
Wood anemone (*Anemone nemorosa*) growing in a hedge forming the parish boundary between Wymondham and Great Melton in central Norfolk.

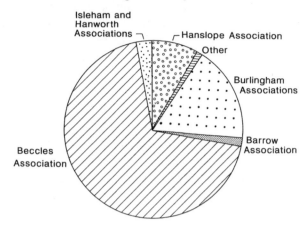

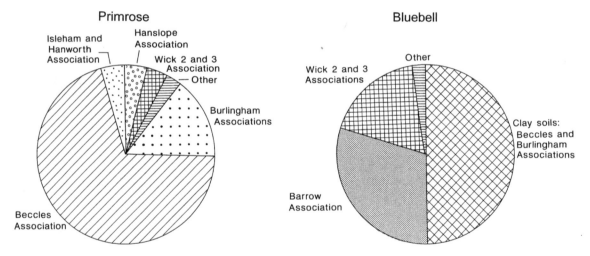

words, a function of landscape history? Or is it a simple consequence of the fact that they will not thrive in dry, leached, environments?

The survey evidence suggests that soil type is, to a significant extent, a *direct* influence on the distribution of these plants, especially in the case of dog's mercury. In Stratton Strawless to the north of Norwich, for example, dog's mercury is absent from all hedges in the centre and south of the parish, including the magnificent hedge on the southern parish boundary (also the hundred boundary between South Erpingham and Taverham) which in other respects appears to be of 'woodland relic' type, containing great stands of maple and hornbeam. The soils here largely fall within the Wick 2 association, being droughty and freely draining. In the north of the parish, however, the ground falls away towards a tributary of the river Bure, and the soils are moister. Here, dog's mercury is present in a number of hedges, but not with any clear preferences for antiquity or origins. At least one is a ruler-straight boundary which is evidently of eighteenth- or nineteenth-century date. In

FIGURE 38.
The distribution of the three main 'woodland relic' herbs in Norfolk hedges, by soil type. Dog's mercury and primrose are largely restricted to the clay soils of the Beccles, Burlingham and Hanslope associations; bluebell is found more widely, also occurring with some frequency on the mildly acidic soils of the Wick and Barrow associations.

nearby Haveringland, where dry acid soils of the Newport 3 association dominate the parish, mixed and species-rich hedges again contain no dog's mercury,
and very little primrose or bluebell, with one notable exception. This is where
a lane, bounded by substantial banks, runs downhill onto lower and damper
ground, corresponding with a small patch of heavy Beccles 3 association soils
beside a tributary of the river Wensum. In the parish of Gresham in the north
of the county, similarly, dog's mercury is absent from most of the higher
ground, which is dominated by Wick 2 soils, but appears sporadically in
hedges on lower, wetter ground, and also in those growing on a very limited
deposit of Beccles association soils. Particularly telling is the evidence from a
number of hedges on the dry Wick 2 and 3 association soils in north-central
Norfolk – in the parishes of Binham, Briston and Corpusty – which contain
that quintessential 'woodland relic' shrub species, small-leafed lime, yet no
dog's mercury or other woodland herbs. There are, it is true, some hedges
which contain dog's mercury on such freely draining soils – even on those of
the particularly light and acid Newport 4 association. But on the whole it is
clear that the distribution of this plant, and also that of primrose, is to a large
extent a direct function of soil type, both plants simply doing significantly
better on moist and calcareous soils than on dry and acid ones. To some extent
the same appears to be true of bluebell, which occurs only sporadically in even
the oldest hedges on the driest soils.

Yet if dog's mercury, primrose and bluebell are poor indicators of 'woodland relic' hedges on lighter and more leached soils they are also – for rather
different reasons – equally unreliable on the heavier clays. Although dog's
mercury, in particular, is often described as a 'slow coloniser' the survey
results leave no doubt that it can spread relatively quickly from woodland or
old hedges, into relatively young ones. This is particularly clear when we
examine hedges planted in the early nineteenth century when clayland
commons were enclosed by parliamentary act, or as the existing pattern of
enclosed fields was being rationalised. Here the rate of progress of dog's
mercury along the hedge, from an earlier boundary where it had long been
present, can be easily measured. In many cases, the plant has progressed 40
metres or more; in the case of one roadside hedge, planted at the enclosure
of Wymondham Common in 1806, it has achieved no less than 115 metres
(perhaps the passage of traffic here has aided dispersal) (TG 124022).
Primrose is even more likely to appear in enclosure hedges in the claylands,
in several cases having spread as much as 100 metres since the early nineteenth century (Figure 39). While it is true to say that neither of these plants
is quite as common in eighteenth- and nineteenth-century hedges as it is in
earlier ones, it is nevertheless clear that the value of either as any kind of
'woodland indicator' is limited. In the well-mapped parish of Morley, for
example, dog's mercury is present in 83 per cent of hedges planted before
1624, in 66 per cent of those planted between 1624 and 1816, but also to
some extent in 50 per cent of those planted since 1816. Evidently, sufficient
reserves of this plant were maintained in woods or hedges on the clays

FIGURE 39.
The hedge was
removed in the 1960s
but dog's mercury and
primrose still grow on
this roadside boundary
in Wymondham,
created by
parliamentary enclosure
in 1811.

throughout the medieval and post-medieval periods to act as a source for neighbouring hedges, into which moist soil conditions encouraged a relatively rapid spread. Much the same appears to be true of primrose, and the presence of one or more of these plants in a particular hedge can thus tell us little or nothing about its history, and certainly does not indicate that it was originally carved out of woodland. On the available evidence bluebells seem so common on both the clays and the light loams of the north-east that their usefulness as a woodland relic indicator also seems doubtful. As already noted, the other woodland relic plants – wood anemone, wood spurge and yellow archangel – are relatively infrequent, even in hedges of great antiquity and potential 'woodland relic' type. In Norfolk, in other words, the distribution of Pollard's 'woodland relic' herbs can tell us comparatively little about the origins of individual hedges.

Turning now to the shrub component, one of the key 'indicators' of 'woodland relic' status – woodland hawthorn, or Midland hawthorn (*Crataegus oxycanthoides*) – was not systematically recorded in the survey, due to the difficulties of distinguishing it in the field from *Crataegus monogyna*, although its presence was noted in a number of south Norfolk hedges. Two other shrubs often considered significant in this respect – small-leafed lime (*Tilia cordata*) and wild service tree (*Sorbus torminalis*) – are, to judge from the results of the survey, both rare in Norfolk hedges. Only 23 occurrences of the former were noted, and a mere five of the latter. In part this may be a result of underrecording, especially of *Sorbus*, but on the whole it seems to reflect a genuine paucity of these plants. Pollard's main criterion of 'woodland relic' status, however, was less the presence of specific rare or infrequent species, more that of the more common woodland shrubs, notably maple, dogwood and hazel, in particularly large quantities, together with a concomitant reduction in the prominence of hawthorn (Pollard 1973). But whichever criteria we employ, it is clear that the results of the Norfolk survey do not really support the idea of 'woodland relic hedges' as a category distinct from 'planted' hedges.

No fewer than 781 hedges were considered to be of 'mixed' character by

FIGURE 40.
Small-leaved lime
(*Tilia cordata*) growing
in an old hedge in
Binham in north
Norfolk.

recorders, in the sense that no single species, or combination of two species, was dominant for the majority of the hedge length. But such hedges were by no means restricted to those with potential woodland origins, or even to ones of any great antiquity. Just under a quarter were on boundaries of 'straight' type, and just over a quarter on ones which, to judge from morphological evidence, were created by piecemeal enclosure. Many of these hedges, however, while evidently 'mixed' in character, were not dominated by those woodland plants noted as important by Pollard – hazel, maple or dogwood – and a better indication of possible 'woodland relic' status is therefore provided by the presence, in a majority of the recorded lengths in a hedge, of at least two of these plants. There were 338 hedges of this type recorded in the county but again, not all were on boundaries with possible woodland origins. While only around 7 per cent were associated with 'straight' boundaries, a high proportion – around 28 per cent – were again associated with ones created by piecemeal enclosure, boundaries which must – by definition – have been planted in areas formerly occupied by arable open fields. The remainder, nearly two-thirds, were indeed associated with boundaries of 'irregular' type, especially roads, parish boundaries and former common edges – features which may well have developed directly from woodland. But such hedges clearly do not constitute anything approaching a distinct, sealed category, separate from hedges planted on formerly open land. Nor do high species counts, it need hardly be said, serve to distinguish a distinct 'woodland relic' group. Of the 373 hedges recorded with an average of six or more species, 6 per cent were associated with 'straight' boundaries, and 19 per cent with ones created by piecemeal enclosure. While the majority of such hedges are thus associated with 'irregular' boundaries, potentially created as woodland was cleared, a substantial minority were again clearly planted within land long cleared of woodland. (Not all hedges containing significant quantities of the main woodland shrubs, it should be emphasised, boast large numbers of species overall. Indeed, the prominence of the key 'woodland' species is sometimes so great that the overall average is brought down below that exhibited by straight, eighteenth- and nineteenth-century hedges in the locality, with great banks of maple, dogwood or hazel occupying five, ten or more metres of the hedge).

Even the small number of records of small-leafed lime were not entirely restricted to boundaries of 'irregular' type (Figure 40). Of the 23 hedges which contained this species, five were created by piecemeal enclosure. Yet it is noteworthy that their distribution corresponds in broad terms with the area (centred on north-central Norfolk) in which this species is especially prominent in ancient woods (Figure 41), although with some significant outliers. In this context, attention should also be drawn to another species. Hornbeam is found in 229 hedges in south and central Norfolk, mainly on the heavier clays but also to some extent on the loams of the Wick associations. Sixty-two per cent of records are from hedges on boundaries of 'irregular' type, mainly on lanes, former common edges and parish boundaries: 25 per cent are on boundaries created by piecemeal enclosure; and only 13 per cent on ones of 'straight'

FIGURE 41.
Records of small-leaved lime (*Tilia cordata*) in Norfolk woods (above) and hedges (below).

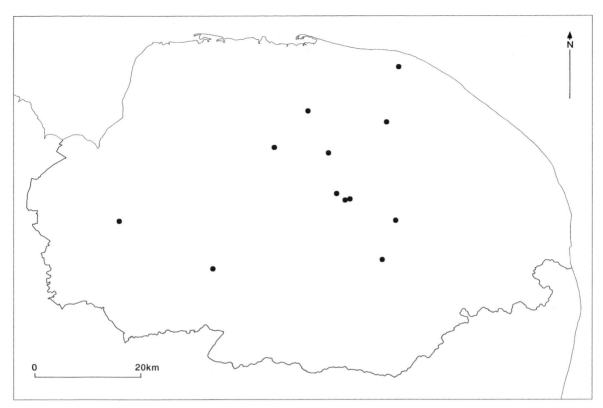

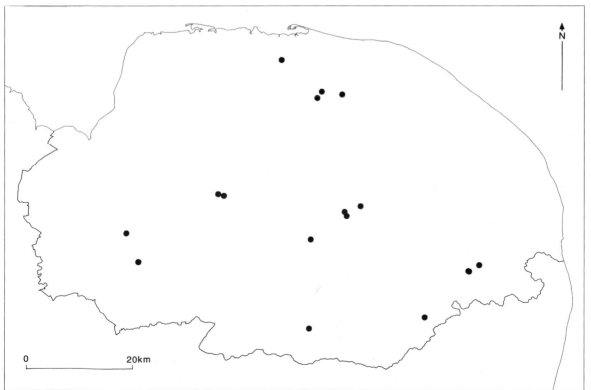

type. Although this species can thus be found growing in hedges planted since *Hedgerow History* c.1700, it is clearly a particular feature of the oldest hedges, as Addington noted as long ago as 1978 in her study of Tasburgh in south Norfolk (Addington 1978, 73). What is particularly interesting is that the distribution of hedges containing hornbeam again broadly corresponds with that of the ancient woods in which the species is today prominent, although extending across a slightly wider area (Figure 42). And in a similar way, while the presence of sessile oak (*Quercus petraea* Leibe) as opposed to pendunculate oak (*Quercus robur*) in hedges was not systematically recorded by the survey, where the distinction was noted the distribution of observations agrees well with the conclusions of E. V. Rogers: sessile oak is thinly scattered in older hedges (especially along roadsides) across north Norfolk from Trunch in the east to Swanton Novers and Glandford in the west, and as far south as Hevingham, Marsham and Ringland, but with particular concentrations around Edgefield and Baconsthorpe. This is the same general area in which this species is well represented in ancient woods (Rogers 1984).

These correspondences are amenable to at least two interpretations. The character of both hedges and woods may reflect variations in the composition of the virgin 'wildwood' in Norfolk, or in that of the modified tracts of wood-pasture that succeeded it, before these were reduced in area during the early Middle Ages by clearance and their surviving fragments managed more intensively as coppiced woodland. Alternatively, the character of the hedges may have been directly affected by variations in the vegetation within the local woods which arose *after* these had become defined and managed. The fact that, in the case of hornbeam and sessile oak, the distribution in hedges is wider than that in woods gives some support to the former explanation.

Some Norfolk hedges, mainly on the claylands in the south and east of the county but also to some extent on the loams of the north and east, thus exhibit the characteristics which Pollard and others have used to define a class of 'woodland relic' hedges, even to the extent of mirroring the character of the vegetation of the local, semi-natural woodland. But the survey results strongly suggest that such hedges cannot, in general, have originated in the manner originally envisaged by Pollard – through the management of the natural vegetation around woodland assarts. Many were evidently planted in late medieval or post-medieval times on land formerly occupied by open-field arable. Even when they are associated with potentially more ancient features of the landscape, these are mainly linear elements like lanes or parish boundaries, rather than the kinds of hedged close which might have been hacked out of the woodland. In part their 'woodland' characteristics must simply arise from the fact that they exist in environments rich in woods and other seed sources, or originally did so. But in part it almost certainly reflects the fact that they were originally planted with a range of species, gathered from the neighbouring woods: it is difficult otherwise to explain why so many of these hedges grow on boundaries of 'piecemeal enclosure' type. As we have already seen, the survey evidence suggests that a high proportion were originally planted

FIGURE 42. Records of hornbeam (*Carpinus betula*) in Norfolk woods (above) and hedges (below).

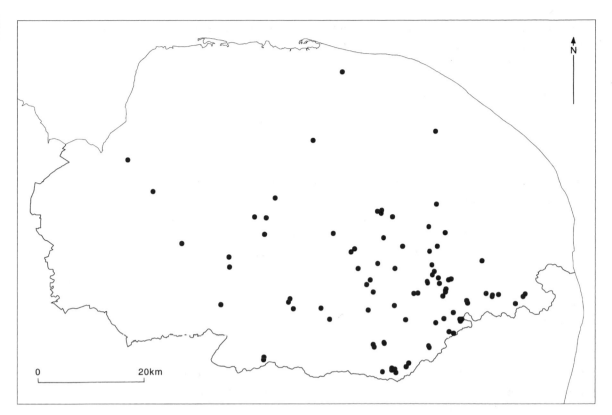

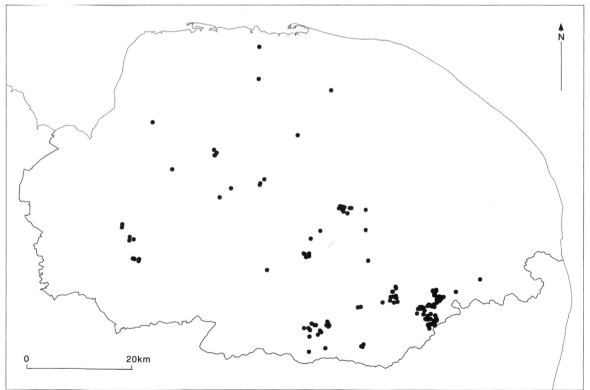

95

with a mixture of species, in contrast to the straight hedges created by parliamentary enclosures, or planted by large landowners in the eighteenth and nineteenth centuries. Where the range of species gathered from local woods and copses by farmers to plant them included rare plants like small-leafed lime or wild service, was sufficiently extensive, and/or was further augmented by colonisation from abundant proximate seed sources, then even relatively recent hedges could evidently take on a 'woodland relic' appearance. Hooper and Pollard rightly suggested at one point that some 'woodland relic' hedges may have originated in this way (rather than by direct management of the existing woodland flora) (Pollard *et al.* 1974, 98), but this in itself rather dissolves the theoretical distinction between their first category of hedges, those with woodland relic origins, and their third, those planted with a number of species.

Conclusion

The Norfolk survey results thus confirm, in broad terms, Hooper's suggestion that older hedges generally have more species than younger ones, while at the same time showing very clearly – as a number of previous studies have done – that the correlation is a weak one and not necessarily linear in character. Multi-species planting, variations in seed supply, and the fact that colonisation rates are higher on some soils than on others, all ensure that hedges of similar age and origins can display wide variation in the kinds, and numbers, of shrub species which they contain. As a tool for assessing even the general age of an individual hedge the 'Hooper method' is thus, without question, of little if any use. The results of the survey offer some, albeit qualified, support for the concept of 'woodland relic' hedges. The distribution of the key ground flora species, especially dog's mercury, appears to be related mainly to soils rather than to hedges with particular origins. But the distribution of the particular shrubs, and combinations of shrubs, highlighted by Pollard as significant in this respect does seem to indicate that certain hedges originated in particularly wooded environments, although probably not usually through the direct management of the woodland understorey. Most were probably planted, some perhaps quite late in the post-medieval period, using a range of suitable shrubs gathered from local woods or hedges. Above all, the survey results highlight the importance of soil type as a factor in variations in hedge flora, both indirectly – through landscape and agrarian history, and thus the character of seed supply and, perhaps, local tenurial structures – and directly – through soil moisture and fertility. The different soil regions and landscape regions of Norfolk thus have their own particular hedgerow histories, and it is to a fuller investigation of these that we must now turn.

CHAPTER FIVE

Hedges and Regional Character

So far we have analysed the characteristics of Norfolk hedges largely in terms of the soils on which they grow. But the various landscape regions of Norfolk are not simply reducible to soils – they do not correspond to single, undifferentiated soil types. Instead they usually comprise a number of different kinds of soil, interdigitated in complex ways. In the discussion that follows we will consider each of the county's main landscape regions in turn, and discuss how their hedges have developed over time.

Ancient countryside: the southern claylands

In historical terms the landscape of the boulder clays of central and southern Norfolk was intimately structured by its complex soil patterns. Open fields were most extensive, and lasted longest, on the lighter soils of the Burlingham 1 and 3 associations, found on the sloping sides of the valleys cutting through the clay plateau; woods and, in particular, commons were especially characteristic of the heavier plateau soils of the Beccles 3 association. Open fields were also extensive on these latter soils, but some enclosed fields were also present from an early date. Kimberley Park, to the north of Wymondham, contains some of the oldest surviving oak trees in the county, mainly pollards but with some standards, many of which are probably of fourteenth- or fifteenth-century date (Figure 43). They are associated with low earthworks defining a pattern of medieval closes, evidently – to judge from their shape – directly reclaimed from the 'wastes' rather than enclosed piecemeal from open fields (Figure 44). Such irregular fields have, in themselves, generally disappeared from the landscape through field 'rationalisation' in comparatively modern times, although some of their constituent hedges remain: nineteenth-century maps show numerous examples, especially in the centre of the county, often close to the edges of woodland. For the most part, however, even the heavier clays seem to have been dominated in medieval times by open fields, to judge from early maps of places like Tittleshall, Godwick, Morley or Raveningham (NRO MS 21129, 179X4; NRO Raynham Box 9b, 27.11.80, R152C; NRO PD3/108(H); private collection); and the majority of field boundaries, therefore, are of late medieval or post-medieval date, and grow in areas in which open fields or commons once existed. The exceptions – boundaries which potentially originated within a once more densely wooded landscape – are mainly on roadsides, former common edges, and parish boundaries.

No fewer than 1,385 hedges were recorded from the boulder clays – around 49 per cent of the total sample, reflecting the large proportion of the county occupied by this formation. Of these, the majority – 894 – were from the heavy Beccles 3 association soils, with 439 from the Burlingham soils and 52 from those of the more calcareous Hanslope association, which occupies limited areas in the far south of the county.* The hedges on all these soils are, compared with those found elsewhere in the county, species-rich. Those on the Hanslope soils have an average of 5.3 species per thirty metres, those on the Beccles soils 5, while those on the Burlingham associations have 4.3; the overall average, across all these soil types, being 5.

The hedges growing on what are potentially the oldest boundaries – that is, those on 'irregular' features like roads and parish boundaries – are, as we might expect, generally of mixed character, and often fall into Hooper and Pollard's 'woodland relic' category. This is probably due to a number of factors: they were planted with useful materials gathered from the local woods; they have existed for a very long time in an environment containing numerous seed sources; and these moist and generally fertile soils encourage high rates of colonisation and retention, and are favourable to a wide range of species. Hawthorn, while almost invariably present in such hedges, is only one among many components: 53 per cent of these hedges were recorded as 'mixed', most of the others were dominated not by hawthorn but by a mixture of hawthorn and blackthorn, or by blackthorn alone. No less than 34 per cent contained six or more species per thirty metres, and 4.5 percent contained eight or more. The average number of species is, however, only 5.1: this is because in many hedges species other than hawthorn dominate for limited lengths. Maple,

* Other areas of Beccles and Burlingham Association soils, the reader should note, are found in the west of the county, associated with Gault clay: see pages 45 and 46.

FIGURE 43.
Ancient oaks in Kimberley Park, central Norfolk, growing on the earthworks of old field boundaries. Some of the trees are of late medieval date.

FIGURE 44.
opposite top
The association of veteran trees and earthworks of old field boundaries in Kimberley Park. The size and shape of the fields indicates that they were reclaimed directly from the waste and were not enclosed piecemeal from open fields.

FIGURE 45.
An elm-invaded hedge at Kirstead, south Norfolk. Vigorous suckering has converted an ancient, species-rich hedge into one dominated almost exclusively by elm.

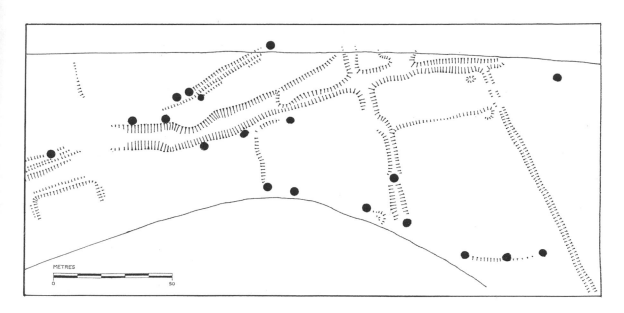

hazel, and dogwood can all form large stands, apparently having out-competed neighbours: 31 per cent of these hedges contained at least two of these key 'woodland' shrubs in a majority of recorded lengths. In others, blackthorn or elm have similarly, but often more systematically, displaced competitors: both are noted for their ability to gradually dominate lengths of hedge through vigorous suckering (Figure 45). There is no very obvious pattern in the extent

to which these old hedges have lost, rather than acquired, species in this way, although there are signs that hedges on the more sandy areas of clay soil are especially prone to this kind of displacement and monopolisation. Patterns of past management – the extent to which hedges have been managed through vigorous coppicing, for example – may also be a factor, together with whether elm was planted as a timber tree, or as part of the hedge, in the first place. Either way, the tendency for old hedges to lose as well as gain species is one of the reasons (as Muir pointed out long ago: 1996, 60) that the age/species number correlation must be more complex, and less direct, than Hooper and his colleagues originally envisaged. Most of these 'irregular' hedges contain dog's mercury or other woodland herbs, and a fifth contain hornbeam, lime or both. Hazel is particularly common, present in 66 per cent.

Some variations in the character of these 'irregular' clayland hedges are clearly related to soil type. Dog's mercury is much rarer in hedges on Burlingham soils than on those of the Beccles 3 association. Dogwood, which prefers moist soils, is also less common on Burlingham soils and holly, which prefers more acidic conditions, is more so (Figure 46). Other variations, however, may have an historical significance. Most of the commons shown on seventeenth- and eighteenth-century maps had curving, convex outlines, funnelling into the points where roads enter them. But some had more rectilinear boundaries, sometimes defining what appear to be later encroachments or intrusions. One example, to the north of Wymondham (TG129047), is today defined by a hedge which, while containing a fair mix of woody species, is largely dominated by blackthorn and, unusually for an old hedge on Beccles association soils, completely lacks dog's mercury in its accompanying ground flora. It is thus very different from another curving former common edge which also survives nearby. This is dominated by dogwood and maple, and contains an abundance of dog's mercury and primrose (TG 118042). The second of these hedges was, perhaps, planted when the common was first defined, and when it still carried a fair amount of tree cover: as one of the authors has argued elsewhere (Barnes 2003), many of Norfolk's clayland commons probably comprised areas of common woodland or wood-pasture well into the medieval period. The other, in contrast, was probably established at a later date, around a large encroachment made at a time when the common in question had already largely degenerated, through the pressure of grazing, to open pasture.

In the thirteenth century most of the claylands seem to have been relatively sparsely hedged, with large areas of open fields within a framework of partly hedged roads, and with extensive commons bounded by hedges and ditches. From the late fourteenth century, however, and probably at an increasing rate from the fifteenth, the open fields were enclosed piecemeal, a process largely completed on the Beccles soils by the mid seventeenth century, and on the lighter Burlingham soils by the mid eighteenth (Skipper 1989). The hedges on these piecemeal enclosure boundaries have on average virtually the same number of species as those in the 'irregular' group, and around the same proportion were considered to be 'mixed' in character by recorders. Indeed,

FIGURE 46.
The frequency of shrubs in the three main forms of hedge growing on the soils of the Norfolk claylands (only those species present in more than 5 per cent of hedges are shown separately).

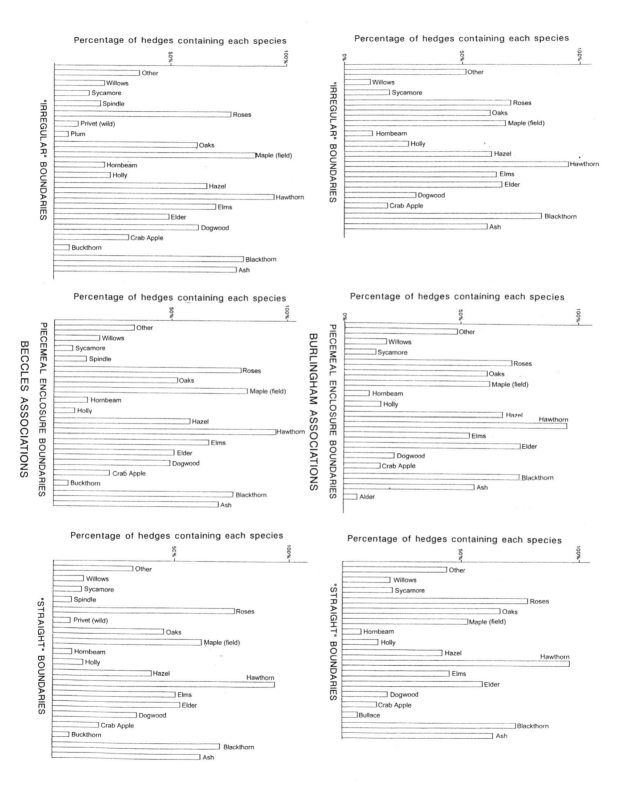

Percentage of hedges containing each species

"IRREGULAR" BOUNDARIES

50% — 100%

Other
Willows
Sycamore
Spindle
Roses
Privet (wild)
Plum
Oaks
Maple (field)
Hornbeam
Holly
Hazel
Hawthorn
Elms
Elder
Dogwood
Crab Apple
Buckthorn
Blackthorn
Ash

Percentage of hedges containing each species

"IRREGULAR" BOUNDARIES

0% — 50% — 100%

Other
Willows
Sycamore
Roses
Oaks
Maple (field)
Hornbeam
Holly
Hazel
Hawthorn
Elms
Elder
Dogwood
Crab Apple
Blackthorn
Ash

Percentage of hedges containing each species

PIECEMEAL ENCLOSURE BOUNDARIES
BECCLES ASSOCIATIONS

50% — 100%

Other
Willows
Sycamore
Spindle
Roses
Oaks
Maple (field)
Hornbeam
Holly
Hazel
Hawthorn
Elms
Elder
Dogwood
Crab Apple
Buckthorn
Blackthorn
Ash

Percentage of hedges containing each species

PIECEMEAL ENCLOSURE BOUNDARIES
BURLINGHAM ASSOCIATIONS

0% — 50% — 100%

Other
Willows
Sycamore
Roses
Oaks
Maple (field)
Hornbeam
Holly
Hazel
Hawthorn
Elms
Elder
Dogwood
Crab Apple
Blackthorn
Ash
Alder

Percentage of hedges containing each species

"STRAIGHT" BOUNDARIES

50% — 100%

Other
Willows
Sycamore
Spindle
Roses
Privet (wild)
Oaks
Maple (field)
Hornbeam
Holly
Hazel
Hawthorn
Elms
Elder
Dogwood
Crab Apple
Buckthorn
Blackthorn
Ash

Percentage of hedges containing each species

"STRAIGHT" BOUNDARIES

50% — 100%

Other
Willows
Sycamore
Roses
Oaks
Maple (field)
Hornbeam
Holly
Hazel
Hawthorn
Elms
Elder
Dogwood
Crab Apple
Bullace
Blackthorn
Ash

taken as a whole the floristic differences between the two groups negligible, the most noticeable being a slightly lower frequency of dogwood, holly, spindle and hornbeam in the piecemeal enclosure hedges. Some examples of the latter are, indeed, relatively species-poor, but as a group these hedges appear similar if not identical to those in the 'irregular' category, experiencing (for example) a similar degree of 'invasion' by elm and sloe, and on the basis of composition alone no individual example could be assigned with confidence to either group. As already noted, so great are the similarities that – coupled with the relatively recent, sixteenth- or seventeenth-century date of most of these hedges – there seems little doubt that the majority were originally planted with a mixture of species.

A surprising number of clayland boundaries, however, are neither of 'irregular' form, nor display the sinuous profiles and other features indicative of piecemeal enclosure, but are instead ruler-straight in character. They fall into two main categories. Some were created by relatively recent planned enclosure: as we have seen, the vast majority of the clayland commons disappeared rapidly in the first two decades of the nineteenth century, almost invariably through parliamentary acts, and were divided by neat meshes of hedges. The high prices of the Napoleonic War years, together with the widespread adoption of under-drainage, sealed the fate of a resource already under threat from agricultural, social and tenurial change – especially the decline of small owner-occupiers, and the development of a more arable economy in the region. But not all of these ruler-straight boundaries were, in spite of appearances, created by enclosure commissioners. Some were laid out within areas already long enclosed, as part of a widespread reorganisation of existing field patterns which occurred across much of England at this time (see page 19). Randall Burroughes of Wymondham, an energetic 'improver' who farmed a substantial holding of over 300 acres, described the systematic transformation of the local landscape in his farming journal, which spans the years 1794–9 (Wade Martins and Williamson 1996). Every winter his men were employed stubbing out hedges and taking down old pollards. In the last two weeks of 1794, for example, Burroughes described how 'Elmer & Meadows began to through down & level an old bank in part of the pasture between little Bones & Maids Yards'; reported that 'the men were employ'd in stubbing a tree or two for firing & other odd jobs'; described how 'some ash timber' was cut down; and how 'the frost continued very severe so much so that ... the men employed in throwing down old hedgerows found the greatest difficulty in penetrating the ground with pick axes'. Often hedges were removed entirely, as small pasture fields were converted into large arable closes. But sometimes thick, outgrown hedges were hacked out and replaced with others, straighter and neater in form. In May 1796, for example, two of his workers were 'employ'd this week in securing the Brickkiln fence against the common sheep by lining the bank under the spring with small thorns and brambles ... and also reclipping the new fenc'd fence west of Burfields' (Wade Martins and Williamson 1996, 81). Cartographic evidence makes it clear that reorganisation of field

FIGURE 47.
An early nineteenth-century hedge at Wymondham in Norfolk. Originally planted with hawthorn, it is now dominated by ash.

FIGURE 48.
A ruler-straight hedge planted in the nineteenth century on the Raveningham estate, on the claylands of south Norfolk. Identical in appearance to hedges established when the local commons were enclosed by parliamentary act, this in fact results from the reorganisation of field boundaries on land that had long been enclosed. Such changes were common in Norfolk in the eighteenth and nineteenth centuries, especially where the land was owned by large landed estates.

boundaries continued on some scale on the claylands through the middle and later decades of the nineteenth century.

Whether created by parliamentary enclosure, or by the 'improvement' of an existing field pattern, these relatively recent clayland hedges are surprisingly varied in composition. Most are dominated by hawthorn, some by a mixture of hawthorn and blackthorn – some indeed, look as if they may originally have been planted with both species. But in addition, while noticeably less mixed than other clayland hedges, they generally contain more species than hedges of similar age on the light lands in the west of the county. The 365 examples examined have an average of 4.2 species per thirty metres and nearly 13 per cent boast an average of 6 or more. Indeed, over a quarter (27 per cent) were considered by recorders to be of 'mixed' character. They typically feature large quantities of ash, rose and elm, but many have significant amounts of maple and a surprising number also include scattered examples of such 'slow-colonising' species as dogwood, spindle, guelder rose and hazel (Figure 46). The high frequency of maple is especially noteworthy, given that this species is often assumed to be a slow coloniser, typical of 'Tudor and earlier' hedges (Rackham 1986, 203).

In general, such hedges seem to be most dominated by hawthorn and blackthorn, and most species-poor, where they have been planted towards the centre of the larger commons. They are most species-rich towards the periphery of such commons, where only small commons were enclosed, or on boundaries newly established within long-enclosed land. Some extreme cases make the point well. When one of the commons in the north of the parish of Wymondham were enclosed in 1806, a new road was laid out which first ran across it, and then for a while parallel to the old common edge (TG 118042). The hedges flanking the first section of this road are clearly dominated by hawthorn, but also contain quantities of rose, ash and blackthorn. The new hedge planted parallel to the old common edge, in contrast, contains large amounts of dogwood and maple, has an average of seven species in each thirty-metre length, and is in most respects indistinguishable from the species-rich hedge marking the common edge itself, which is on the opposite side of the same road. Most of the variation in composition and character displayed by these relatively recent hedges is thus related to seed supply. Those examples planted nearest to woods or existing hedges are, on the whole, richer than those in more isolated locations. But soils and topography have also played their part. Ruler-straight eighteenth- and nineteenth-century hedges on Beccles 3 association soils thus tend to have slightly more species (4.3) than those on soils of the Burlingham associations (4.2), while those in damp hollows fed by watercourses from adjoining (long-enclosed) higher ground are also noticeably richer than their neighbours. A few hedges seem to break these broad rules, however, appearing more species-rich than expected, given their location. In some cases it is likely that multi-species planting, particularly of hawthorn/blackthorn/ash mixes, continued into relatively recent times, on smaller owner-occupied farms.

These relatively recent hedges seem to have been particularly susceptible to colonisation by ash and sycamore, the latter evidently quite widely planted as a timber tree on the claylands at this time. In a number of cases, these species have extensively invaded, in some instances giving rise to almost pure ash or sycamore hedges (Figure 47). It is noteworthy that the older clayland hedges have seldom, if ever, been extensively colonised by either plant in this way. Observations of modern growth patterns suggest that if ash and sycamore are already present in a hedge, then management by vigorous coppicing can increase their representation. The difference between older and newer clayland hedges in this respect may perhaps indicate that while most pre-eighteenth-century hedges were managed by plashing in their early years, later ones were generally coppiced throughout their life. It is also noteworthy that the slow-colonising dogwood is surprisingly well represented in these recent clayland hedges, especially in those created where commons were enclosed. It is possible that the plant may have been growing on some commons before these were enclosed and ploughed and the hedges planted: this species regenerates readily from the rootstock. Another possibility is that the seeds had been brought down by watercourses into the shallow depressions in which many clayland commons were located, from older hedges on the surrounding higher ground.

Examining the species composition of clayland hedges makes more obvious certain things which are in any case suggested by topographic approaches. In particular, it highlights the fact that hedges on parish boundaries, former common edges, and along roadsides are generally of greater antiquity than those which simply bound fields. At the same time it demonstrates that the term 'ancient countryside', so often used for this kind of landscape, can in some ways be misleading. Not only were large areas of new fields created by the enclosure of commons in the decades around 1800 but, especially where large estates owned much of the land, many other new hedges were created through the comprehensive reorganisation of the existing field pattern. The countryside around places like Kimberley, Great Melton, or Raveningham is dominated by ruler-straight hedges, relatively species-poor in character (Figure 48). Even where the boundaries themselves were not radically changed or realigned, the hedges growing on them were sometimes systematically replanted. This is particularly evident on the Raveningham estate, where species-poor hedges on roads to the east of the park have ancient oaks standing on the *opposite* side of the associated ditch, evidently marking the line of the original hedges, which had been removed in the eighteenth or nineteenth centuries. Such large-scale reorganisations of the field pattern have been noted by researchers in a number of areas of England, including Shropshire (Cameron and Pannet 1980a, 147) and Cornwall (Turner 2004).

One factor which clearly distinguishes eighteenth- and nineteenth-century clayland hedges from those planted in earlier periods is the character of the trees growing within them. 'Irregular' hedges, and those created by piecemeal enclosure, still often contain old pollards (Figures 49 and 50). The majority are oaks, but there are scattered examples of ash and hornbeam, a number of

FIGURE 49.
Pollarded oak in an
ancient hedge in
Kenninghall, south
Norfolk.

FIGURE 50.
Two huge pollarded
oaks remain in this
field boundary at
Wreningham even
though the
accompanying hedge
was removed long ago.

long-dead elms, and a few examples of maple, as at Kirstead (Figures 51 and 52). Virtually no hedges planted in the period after 1700 contain pollards, and some of the few exceptions seem to have incorporated free-standing trees which had been growing on commons *before* enclosure. As we have seen (see page 19), the eighteenth century saw increasing hostility to pollarding on the part of large landowners, so this absence is perhaps unsurprising. Landowners instead chose to plant standard trees, mainly oaks but sometimes elm, ash and sycamore. Large numbers of trees of all kinds have, however, disappeared in the course of the twentieth century. Clayland hedges which are now quite denuded of significant timber are often shown as richly studded with trees on the Ordnance Survey First Edition six inch maps of the late nineteenth century.

The north-eastern loams

In some ways the landscape history of north-eastern Norfolk – dominated by the dry but fertile soils of the Wick 3 association and the more acidic, less fertile soils of the Wick 2 association, and interspersed with ribbons of low-lying ground characterised by the damp, peaty soils of the Hanworth association – parallels that of the southern claylands. However, there are important differences. In north-eastern Norfolk, the dominance of open fields was greater in the Middle Ages: indeed, apart from closes in the immediate vicinity of settlements, and the commons around which most settlements clustered, most of the land was occupied by open arable. Here, too, we can make the same morphological distinction between 'irregular' boundaries, those created by piecemeal enclosure, and ruler-straight examples of eighteenth- and nineteenth-century date. But the latter form of boundary is more common in this district than on the claylands, for two reasons. In a number of parishes open fields were not largely or entirely removed by early piecemeal enclosure but instead remained extensive into the later eighteenth century, and were only then finally enclosed by parliamentary acts. This was true of much of the 'island' of Flegg, and also of the land lying immediately to the west of the Halvergate marshes, between Acle and Norwich, where William Faden's county map of 1797 notes, in several places, the continuing existence of 'common fields'. But in addition, on the Wick 2 soils especially, medium-sized landed estates (and some large ones, such as Gunton and Wolterton) were far more prominent than on the clays, and the extent to which the existing field pattern was comprehensively reorganised in the course of the eighteenth and nineteenth centuries was correspondingly greater. William Marshall, writing of this district in 1787, noted 'a practice, which at present prevails, of grubbing up old worn-out hedges, and planting new ones', so that a 'new straight hedge is obtained' (Marshall 1787, 111).

Taken as a whole, the hedges of north-east Norfolk display a number of characteristics which distinguish them from those of the claylands, many of which can be directly related to environmental rather than to historical factors. Holly is a much more prominent feature of these hedges, dogwood far less common: both reflect the more acidic and freely draining character of the Wick soils. Similar factors explain more subtle differences, such as the greater incidence of wild cherry and the comparative rarity of buckthorn. The most noticeable difference between the hedges of the two districts, however, relates to the timber species, elm and oak (Figure 53). Oak is much more frequent in north-east Norfolk than on the boulder clays, as a shrub component, as a standard tree and, in older hedges, as a pollard. While in part this may reflect the ease with which oak will colonise hedges on these soils, it also reflects local planting policies, and the evident preference in the district for oak over elm as a hedgerow tree: the latter is much less common than on the clays, especially in the more recent hedges. It is noteworthy than Nathaniel Kent, writing of the area in 1796, described the contemporary practice of piecemeal enclosure in the following terms:

> Whenever a person can get four or five acres together, he plants a whitethorn hedge around it, and *sets an oak* at every rod distance, which is consented to by a kind of general courtesy from one neighbour to another … (Kent 1796, 72; our italics).

Another distinguishing feature of hedges in the district is that many grow on substantial banks, which rise very steeply from the surrounding fields; these are frequently a metre or more in height (Figure 54). Although many of the older hedges elsewhere in the county are associated with banks, these are generally less massive and less vertical in character, and probably result simply from the repeated clearing-out of the adjacent ditch. Many examples in the north-east, in contrast, were evidently constructed at the time of planting, in part by scraping up soil from the surrounding fields. Marshall, in the late eighteenth century, described the local practice of planting hedges on banks 'perhaps two feet above the level of the adjoining enclosure' (Marshall 1787, 103–4). Such hedges made good initial progress because the 'loose made ground' of the bank served to retain moisture well, an important consideration on these dry soils. But Marshall believed that the hedge's later development was hampered by the erosion of the bank and the exposure of roots. Towards the coast such banks are often topped by only a thin and intermittent line of vegetation, presumably due to the effect of prolonged exposure to the salt winds. This is not a recent development; Marshall noted these 'mere mud walls' as a particular feature of the district. He also mentions one other characteristic of the district's boundaries: the sporadic planting of hedges of furze, or gorse (*Ulex europaeus*) (Marshall 1787, 110). Usually gorse was used to protect a new hawthorn hedge but on the poorest soils it was occasionally employed as a hedging plant in its own right. Few examples survive today, the best perhaps being those along Spa Lane in Aylsham, to the east of Frog Hall (TG 173250).

In this district the 'irregular' hedges – mainly on roadsides, parish boundaries, and dividing areas of low-lying meadow from arable – are noticeably less species-rich than those on the clays, with an average of only 3.7 species per thirty metres. Moreover, dog's mercury and primrose are very restricted in their distribution, limited to pockets of clay, or to the damp, low-lying soils of the Hanworth association. Bluebells, conversely, are more common. Hornbeam is found on only a handful of occasions and, in general, fewer hedges were considered to be 'mixed' in character by recorders. While in part these features may again be a function of soil conditions, they must also reflect aspects of the district's landscape history, and in particular the history of woodland clearance. This was a densely-settled area in medieval times, and while Domesday records a number of large areas of woodland here (and the evidence of place-names suggests even more extensive tracts earlier in the Saxon period) medieval maps and documents generally portray a poorly wooded landscape. In this context it is noticeable that hazel can be found in around 36 per cent of hedges growing on 'irregular' boundaries, less than on the clays but suggesting nevertheless that some of these features may have come into existence when significant amounts of woodland existed in the district and that they are, therefore, of some considerable antiquity. It is also noteworthy that elm, while in general poorly represented in the district's hedges, is reasonably common in hedges of irregular type. It is thus possible that elm is, in this area, a 'woodland relic' species, which has suckered into hedges from long-lost areas of woodland or wood-pasture. It is also possible, however, that the greater frequency of the species in these older hedges simply reflects changes in planting preferences over time, from elm to oak. Cameron and Pannet similarly noted the high frequency of elm (in this case, *Ulmus glabra*) in 'woodland relic' hedges in Warwickshire (Cameron and Pannet 1980a, 151).

As on the claylands, the piecemeal enclosure hedges are, as a group, virtually indistinguishable from those growing on 'irregular' boundaries, suggesting once again that most were planted with a range of species, including in particular maple and holly. And once again they clearly form a category distinct from the 'straight' hedges of post-1700 enclosure, which are overwhelmingly dominated by hawthorn and oak, with much ash and rose, but with only small quantities of hazel, holly and maple. The average number of species in such hedges – 2.6 – is noticeably lower than for similar hedges on the claylands, probably reflecting both the freely draining character of the local soils and a relative paucity of seed sources in what had, by the eighteenth century, become a very sparsely wooded district.

Planned countryside: the light lands of the north and west

On the face of it the hedges of the light land districts of northern and western Norfolk – mostly, as we have seen, created by the enclosure of open fields, heaths and sheepwalks in the course of the eighteenth and nineteenth centuries – should offer little of interest to the landscape historian. But these boundaries have, in spite of their relative modernity, considerable historical and cultural importance, associated as they are with the landscapes forged by the 'Agricultural Revolution', a movement with which this district – and in particular the great 'improving' estates of Holkham and Houghton – was intimately

FIGURE 51.
An unusual example of
a pollarded hornbeam
in a hedge in Kirstead,
south Norfolk.

FIGURE 52.
opposite
Although the
overwhelming majority
of old pollards in
Norfolk hedges are
oaks, other species once
managed in this way
are sporadically found.
A fine pollarded maple
at Kirstead, south
Norfolk.

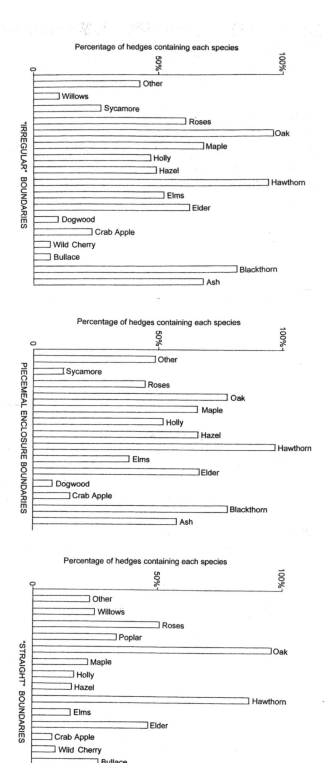

Percentage of hedges containing each species

"IRREGULAR" BOUNDARIES

Percentage of hedges containing each species

PIECEMEAL ENCLOSURE BOUNDARIES

Percentage of hedges containing each species

"STRAIGHT" BOUNDARIES

FIGURE 53.
The frequency of the principal shrub species in the three main forms of hedge (those of 'irregular' form, those created by piecemeal enclosure, and those growing on straight boundaries) in north-east Norfolk. Most are on the well-drained loams of the Wick associations. (Only those species present in more than 5 per cent of hedges are shown separately.)

connected. They also pose their own particular problems of interpretation, and display their own distinctive character.

We may begin by considering those hedges found in the 'Good Sands' district of north-west Norfolk: low, rolling chalk uplands which are cut by a number of major valleys and which fall away northwards and westwards, towards the sea. The higher ground is covered by sandy drift, giving rise to the droughty, acidic soils of the Barrow association. Much of this area was, before the eighteenth century, occupied by grass heath, although large areas of arable also existed (Wade Martins and Williamson 1999, 9–12). The latter were farmed from villages associated with small areas of glacial clay which, carrying a perched water table, could provide necessary drinking water for humans and livestock, otherwise difficult to obtain in these dry uplands. The lower slopes, falling towards rivers and the sea, are occupied by the kinder soils of the Newmarket 2 association, more calcareous in character but dry and, once again, liable to leach nutrients rapidly. Before the eighteenth century these soils were largely occupied by open-field arable, with some areas of calcareous heath and other grazing. Northwards, the Newmarket soils give way on lower ground to coastal alluvium. But to the west there is a more complicated situation, for here rocks older than the chalk, lying at the base of the denuded escarpment, are exposed, while wide valleys form an extension of the Fen basin. The result is a strip of very varied soils, formed in small areas of clay (Burlingham and Beccles associations), tracts of acid sands (Newport 4 association), and extensive areas of peaty deposits (Isleham association).

Hedges have survived well on the drift-covered 'uplands', mainly because much of the land here has remained in the hands of large estates like Houghton and Holkham. They are almost universally species-poor, with an average of only three species (including planted timber) per thirty metres. Of the 117 hedges sampled on the Barrow association soils, 45 per cent had fewer than three species, 43 per cent between three and four species, and only 12 per cent more than four. Hawthorn is the overwhelmingly dominant plant, accompanied to varying extents by those by now familiar 'rapid colonisers' – elder, rose, ash and blackthorn – together with some oak (mainly in the form of standard trees), a little maple and elm, and small quantities of crab, hazel, sycamore, privet, dogwood and holly (Figure 55). Other species are also present, but only in less than 5 per cent of the sampled hedges.

As in other regions, there is some correlation between age and diversity. As we have seen (above, pp. 79–80), the holdings of the Houghton estate in the parishes of Houghton, Harpley and Rudham were mapped in 1720 and again in 1836. At the former date the landscape was still largely unenclosed, but by the latter it mainly (although still not completely) lay in hedged fields (Houghton Hall archives, maps 1 and 21). The map of 1720 shows a mere 5 per cent of the hedges with fewer than three species which were recorded in the survey, but 12 per cent of those with 3–4 species, 20 per cent of those with more than four, and all those (a mere nine, admittedly) with more than five. Hedges of 'mixed' character make up 38 per cent of the pre-1720 hedges but

only 7 per cent of those planted between 1720 and 1836, and none of those planted after this date. Indeed, the latter – nine in all – are almost pure hawthorn, and among the most species-poor in the county, often containing little else other than oak timber and occasional examples of elder and rose. At the other extreme, hazel and maple, while occurring to some extent in hedges planted between 1720 and 1836, are both much more prominent in the pre-1720 hedges. Hazel is found in 71 per cent of the pre-1720 hedges but in only 20 per cent of those planted between 1720 and 1836, and in none of those planted after 1836; maple occurs in 62 per cent of the pre-1720 hedges, 25 per cent of the 1720–1836 group, and in 11 per cent of the post-1836 examples.

Yet if there is some correlation between species content and age, it is once again a broad one. Not all the mixed and species-rich hedges are found on the earliest boundaries; nor, conversely, do all the pre-1720 boundaries carry mixed or species-rich hedges. Indeed, the majority of the latter (55 per cent) are clearly dominated by hawthorn, and in most cases contain a range of species which is identical to that found in hedges planted in the area in the period up to 1836. And of the 12 per cent of hedges with an average of more than four species per thirty metres, only six are on boundaries which were undoubtedly

FIGURE 54.
Many hedges in north-east Norfolk grow on prominent banks, like this beside an old lane which forms the parish boundary between Sloley and Scottow.

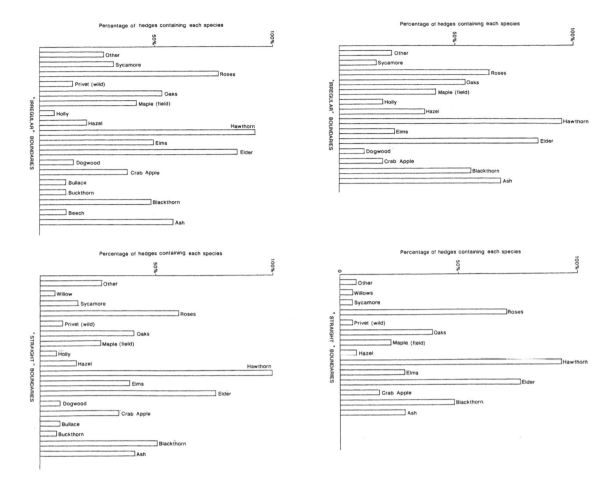

Percentage of hedges containing each species

"IRREGULAR" BOUNDARIES

Other
Sycamore
Roses
Privet (wild)
Oaks
Maple (field)
Holly
Hazel
Hawthorn
Elms
Elder
Dogwood
Crab Apple
Bullace
Buckthorn
Blackthorn
Beech
Ash

Percentage of hedges containing each species

"IRREGULAR" BOUNDARIES

Other
Sycamore
Roses
Oaks
Maple (field)
Holly
Hazel
Hawthorn
Elms
Elder
Dogwood
Crab Apple
Blackthorn
Ash

Percentage of hedges containing each species

"STRAIGHT" BOUNDARIES

Other
Willow
Sycamore
Roses
Privet (wild)
Oaks
Maple (field)
Holly
Hazel
Hawthorn
Elms
Elder
Dogwood
Crab Apple
Bullace
Buckthorn
Blackthorn
Ash

Percentage of hedges containing each species

"STRAIGHT" BOUNDARIES

Other
Willows
Sycamore
Roses
Privet (wild)
Oaks
Maple (field)
Hazel
Hawthorn
Elms
Elder
Crab Apple
Blackthorn
Ash

FIGURE 55.
The frequency of shrub species in the two main forms of hedge (those of 'irregular' form and those growing on straight boundaries) in north-west Norfolk. Above: hedges growing on soils of the Barrow association. Below: hedges growing on soils of the Newmarket association. (Only those species present in more than 5 per cent of hedges are shown separately).

hedged by 1720, against four originating after this date and three of uncertain origins. It is, however, noteworthy that some of the species-poor hedges of pre-1720 date are characterised by massive stools of ash, maple or hawthorn, very different in character to the plants found in the more recent hedges. It should also be noted that all of the hedges with the highest species counts – those containing an average of five species or more per thirty metres – are associated with small areas of damper soil, formed in pockets of glacial clay, within the general matrix of the Barrow association; and that it was in these hedges that the only examples of dog's mercury and primrose were recorded. All this suggests that while *in general* the older hedges of the area contain more species than younger ones, this is not invariably the case; and that the low numbers of shrubs present in the district's hedges is only in part a consequence of their comparative youth. The dry, acidic character of the local soils – other than on the small pockets of damp clay – has evidently retarded the rate at which new plants can successfully colonise. In addition, the marked absence of local trees and woodland, before the large-scale enclosures and afforestation schemes carried out in the eighteenth and nineteenth centuries, ensured that there were few local seed sources.

While the composition of individual hedges cannot be used to date them, the character of the district's hedges reflects its history in more general ways. For example, those few species-rich hedges associated with the small pockets of damper ground contain a range of shrubs and herbs, including hazel and dog's mercury, no different from those found in the older hedges on the main area of boulder clays, in the centre and south of the county. Some woodland must have existed in the immediate vicinity when these hedges were first planted, in spite of the fact that Domesday shows the area as almost completely devoid of woods, and medieval documents present a picture of a bare and treeless landscape. The existence of woodland or wood-pasture on these 'uplands' at an early date is, in fact, also implied by certain local place-names, including those for settlements like Harpley and Choseley (OE *leah*, 'wood' or 'clearing'). A map of North Creake, surveyed in 1624, names the open commons on the higher ground as 'The Frith', from the OE *Frið*, 'a wood' (NRO Diocesan T123A). Not only were some of the bare sheepwalks recorded in later maps and documents thus partially wooded in the early Middle Ages; some of this woodland must have survived up until the time the earliest hedges came into existence.

Other aspects of the district's hedges reflect more recent circumstances. The relative paucity of oak in these hedges, compared with the situation on the north-eastern loams (oak is here the fifth most common species, rather than joint first) probably reflects the fact that whereas the small and medium-sized estates in the latter region tended to plant their timber in hedges, the rather larger estates in this generally less fertile land concentrated theirs in the extensive woods and plantations which are a noticeable feature of the local landscape.

The hedges growing on the lower ground, on the more calcareous Newmarket 2 association soils, are again mainly dominated by hawthorn. Elder is found in 76 per cent of hedges, rose in 62 per cent, blackthorn/bullace in 50 per cent, elm in 42 per cent, oak in 43 per cent and ash in 50 per cent. But in addition to these rapid-colonisers and timber trees, a number of other plants are present in significant quantities, even in relatively species-poor hedges. Crab is present in 35 per cent, maple in 30 per cent, sycamore in 20 per cent and privet in 11 per cent. Yet paradoxically, while a greater *range* of species can be found in these hedges than in those growing on the Barrow association, just discussed, they contain on average rather fewer species in any thirty metre section – only 2.6. The overwhelming majority of hedges (72 per cent) have fewer than three species per thirty metres; 14 per cent have between three and four; and 14 per cent have more than four (Figure 55).

This again is broadly what we would expect, if age were closely related to species content, for the Newmarket soils remained largely unenclosed until the eighteenth century. But closer examination suggests a more complex picture. Here, once again, there are a number of hedges which, although growing on boundaries shown on seventeenth-century maps, have low species counts; and once again these often contain massive stools of ash, hawthorn and occasionally maple. Moreover, as on the drift-covered uplands, the location of the most species-rich hedges – those with more than four species, and especially those with more than five, well-mixed and containing such slow colonisers as hazel – suggests that they are not necessarily the oldest. Indeed, at least 30 per cent of examples are associated with boundaries of known, or probable, eighteenth- or nineteenth-century date. Most are found on the western edge of the main chalk escarpment, on relatively low ground, especially within the parishes of Gayton and Fincham. They are seldom found in the middle of the broad sweeps of open chalk. On this lower ground, as already noted, the calcareous soils of the Newmarket 2 association give way to a diverse and often damper range of soils, formed in pockets of clay and peat. The hedges on these soils are rather different in character from those just discussed. They are noticeably richer, with an average of 3.9 species per thirty metres, as opposed to 2.7. No less than a quarter have more than five species; hazel and maple are much more common, present in 39 per cent and 41 per cent of hedges respectively. These differences seem to be a direct consequence of soil character, for hedges growing on moist soils, as we have seen, generally acquire and retain species at higher rates than those on drier sites. It is possible that these relatively species-rich hedges have in turn acted as a seed source for those growing on the neighbouring areas of chalk soil, increasing their diversity in comparison with those more remotely located, on the higher slopes. But we should also note that, close to this junction of soil types, there are a number of areas of woodland – some ancient, some very early plantations – and these must also have served to increase the seed supply to the neighbouring hedges. The most diverse hedge recorded on the Newmarket 2 soils, in the parish of Gayton, and containing an average of nine species per thirty metres, thus lies next to Soigne Wood (TF 765175). This is an area of early coppiced woodland, and not surprisingly the hedge includes many of the species growing within it.

To the south of the 'Good Sands' lies Breckland, the most agriculturally marginal district in eastern England. Here, as we have seen (page 55), most of the land consisted of heath and open arable before the eighteenth century, except in the immediate vicinity of villages. Some of the area is again characterised by the relatively calcareous soils of the Newmarket 2 association, but large tracts are occupied by the acid sands of the Newport 4, Methwold and Worlington associations. In addition, areas of low-lying, waterlogged soil also occur in the numerous valleys – the peaty Isleham and the sandy Olleton associations. In spite of its late enclosure history, the hedges of the district are rather *less* species-poor than those of north-west Norfolk, with an average of 3.7 species per thirty metres. In part this is due to the fact that those hedges growing on the damp soils of the Isleham and Ollerton associations are richer than others, with four and five species per thirty metres respectively – yet further evidence for the importance of soil moisture content as a determining factor in the species content of hedges. But it is also a consequence of the existence of a scatter of moderately mixed hedges on the other soils, especially close to villages, which contain significant quantities of maple and, to a lesser extent, hazel. These are mostly on the sides of roads, but not always ones of

FIGURE 56.
Lines or 'rows' of Scots pine are a common form of field boundary across much of Breckland. The trees in this example at Gallows Hill, Thetford, are only slightly twisted and were probably managed as a hedge for only a relatively short period of time.

FIGURE 57.
The Scots pines in this roadside 'row' at Cockley Cley have a highly twisted growth pattern: they were managed as a hedge until well into the twentieth century.

FIGURE 58.
One of the few
examples of Scots pines
still maintained as a
recognisable hedge at
Brettenham in south-
west Norfolk.

any great antiquity. The vast majority of the Breckland hedges, however, are as we would expect species-poor, dominated by hawthorn, and contain only small quantities of rapid colonisers (ash, blackthorn, elder, rose) or species planted for timber (oak, elm, sycamore). A significant proportion are elm-invaded. Even some early nineteenth-century hedges have been converted to almost pure lines of elm, the poor, sandy character of the soils evidently encouraging this development.

The most characteristic features of the Breckland landscape, however, are not hedges at all, but rather the lines of Scots pines which border many of the fields. These were already being noted as a distinguishing feature of the area by the late nineteenth century, and accorded their own distinctive name, 'deal rows': 'deal' is the old East Anglian term for any form of conifer. The vast majority are now lines of outgrown trees, often although not invariably with a twisted, slightly contorted form (Figures 56 and 57). But there is no doubt that most, although perhaps not all, were originally planted densely, at intervals of around 0.3 metres, and kept cut and often plashed (to judge from their current growth pattern) at a height of around 1.5 metres. Many continued to be so managed into the twentieth century, most notably on the Cockley Cley estate. Today only a handful of examples are still recognisably hedges, and these mainly in Suffolk. The best Norfolk example is perhaps that bordering the road between Bridgeham and Brettenham (TL940843) (Figure 58). Some of the 'rows' are associated with low banks, but the majority are not.

Pines were presumably chosen as a hedging plant because they will tolerate
the dry, sandy soils of the district better than hawthorn, and rapidly provide
shelter for crops and game. Similar 'rows' can be found, albeit sporadically, in
other sandy areas of southern and eastern England, such as the Suffolk
Sandlings. The few examples still managed as hedges show that, with an effort,
pines can be made to provide a reasonable stockproof barrier. But a very short
period of neglect allows the plants to 'get away', and once grown into trees it
is impossible to return them once more to bushes. As early as 1908
W. G. Clarke noted the start of the decline in regular management, describing
how 'These hedges are made of ordinary trees kept stunted by constant trim-
ming, and many of the lines of fir trees now bordering plantations were
originally hedges, but have ceased to be trimmed' (Clarke 1908, 563–4). In 1925
he implied that many were still being regularly cut, noting how pines were
'still the characteristic tree of the district, planted either in rows known as
'belts', or artificially dwarfed as hedges' (Clarke 1925, 17). Most, according to
local tradition, ceased to be managed during the First or Second World Wars,
when manpower was in short supply. When management ceased the density
of plants was reduced, either naturally (through competition, as individual
trees outgrew their neighbours) or through deliberate thinning.

It is difficult to map the distribution of the 'rows' accurately for a number
of reasons (Figure 59). In many cases, single pine lines have subsequently been
widened to form narrow belts (usually between 10 and 25 m in width) in order
to provide better cover for game. Only detailed examination of such belts,
which are another common feature of the Breckland landscape, would reveal
how many originally comprised single lines of pines. More importantly, many
of the rows now lie buried within, or have been destroyed by, the extensive
pine plantations established by the Forestry Commission in the district in the
1920s and 30s. It is nevertheless clear that these idiosyncratic boundary features
are not found to the same extent throughout Breckland. There are notable
gaps in their distribution, such as that in the area around Mundford, Weeting
and Methwold. Such *lacunae* do not appear to correspond to particular soil
types and may instead reflect the planting policies of particular estates.

It is unclear when pine hedges were first planted in the district. Sussams has
noted how as early as 1668 Thomas Wright described his use of 'Furre-hedges'
to reduce the progress of the famous sand blow that engulfed much of the
parish of Santon Downham (Sussams 1996, 105). Scots pines may indeed be
indigenous to the area. The distinctive assemblages of beetles and fungi associated with them have suggested to some scientists that the species never
entirely died out in East Anglia, as it apparently did elsewhere in lowland
England during the Roman period (Dannatt 1996, 22). Pines are certainly
shown as hedgerow trees on some early maps of Breckland, such as that of the
Walsingham estates in Tottington, surveyed in 1774 (NRO WLS XVII/4).
Some examples referred to in a court case at Merton in 1772 were already 27
feet (8.1 m) high (NRO WLS XXXI/15/1 417X6). But it is nevertheless unlikely
that the pine hedges themselves represent a 'traditional' form of field boundary

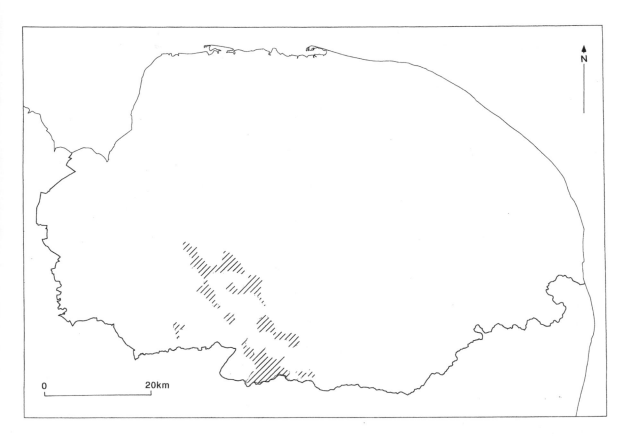

FIGURE 59.
The general
distribution of Scots
pine 'rows' in Norfolk.

in the area. The vast majority grow on straight boundaries of eighteenth- or nineteenth-century origin; the exceptions are on roads which were almost certainly only first hedged in this period. But precisely *when* in the post-1700 period pine hedges became fashionable remains uncertain. The plants themselves offer no real clues. Individual specimens girth slowly while still managed as part of a hedge, and their present circumference is mainly a function of the length of time which has passed since management ceased, and the subsequent spacing of plants within the rows, rather than a direct reflection of age. While hedges of this type may have been planted as early as the seventeenth century, they do not seem to have been common before the nineteenth. They receive no mention from writers like Nathaniel Kent or Arthur Young, the latter in particular usually keen to describe the novel or unusual. Clarke in 1908 was confident that the rows had only been planted on a large scale 'since about 1840' (Clarke 1908, 563), but Bacon in 1884 referred to 'fences of Scotch fir' as if they were a well-established part of the Breckland scene (Bacon 1844, 392). Perhaps the earliest reference comes from David Davey in 1829:

> Within two miles of Brandon I observed a mode, to me at least new, of raising a good fence in a very bad soil; a bank is thrown up, about four or five feet high, and of a considerable thickness at the bottom; upon the top of this is planted a row of Scotch firs, as thick almost as they can stand;

these seem to make rapid progress in this soil and branching out towards the sides, immediately from the ground, and have the additional very strong recommendation of affording the best shelter from storms to the sheep and cattle which are fed, or rather starved upon the land (Blatchley 1982, 136).

On the other hand, it should be noted that some of the rows grow on boundaries which had certainly come into existence before the end of the eighteenth century. Many of those in Cockley Cley, for example, are on boundaries shown on a survey of 1796 (NRO, Norfolk and Norwich Arch. Soc. collection). On balance, the planting of pine hedges probably began on a sporadic basis as early as the seventeenth century, but only became common from the late eighteenth century and reached a peak during the first half of the nineteenth century.

FIGURE 60.
The Duke of Argyll's Tea Plant (*Lycium barbarum*) in a hedge at Hockwold-cum-Wilton. The plant, an introduction from Asia, was widely used for 'gapping up' hedges on the light lands of west Norfolk in the nineteenth century.

Pines were not the only idiosyncratic hedging plant employed by large estates in the eighteenth and nineteenth centuries on the light lands of west Norfolk. Beech was occasionally used in Breckland but of more importance – and also found more widely across the west of the county – is the Duke of Argyll's Tea Plant (*Lycium barbarum*), a species introduced to Britain in the eighteenth century. With its sharp thorns, the plant is well suited for hedging, while its purple flowers have an obvious aesthetic appeal (Figure 60). But few hedges seem to have been originally planted with the species (one on the Holkham estate is a possible exception) and the plant was evidently used in the nineteenth century primarily for 'gapping up' existing hedges. Vigorous suckering has subsequently ensured successful colonisation along lengths of hedge. Particular concentrations of the plant are found around Roudham and Bridgeham, and in Hockwold-cum-Wilton, but there are scattered examples throughout Breckland and, more thinly, across north-west Norfolk.

Lilac (*Syringa vulgaris*) also occurs in a number of Breckland hedges, often dominating long sections to the exclusion of other species (Figure 61). Scattered examples are again found more widely on light, sandy soils across the county, and a few even occur on heavier soils, including a magnificent example at Thurton in south-east Norfolk. But the plant evidently does best on sandier soils (it has also been noted as a distinctive feature of the Sandlings region of eastern Suffolk (Land Use Consultants 1999)). There is no evidence that it was ever deliberately used as a hedging plant. Most if not all examples appear to be the result of colonisation, followed by vigorous suckering, the source of the seeds being local gardens or, in some cases, the understorey of nearby estate woods (one fine hedge in Roudham is, for more than thirty metres, entirely composed of a mixture of lilac and Duke of Argyll's Tea Plant: TF 978898). Snowberry, which is widespread in hedges in the county although again especially in the west, likewise seems to be a colonist from estate woodlands, where it was extensively planted as game cover.

FIGURE 61.
Lilac is an invasive plant which is especially common in hedges on light, sandy soils. An example from Brettenham, south-west Norfolk.

The idiosyncratic planting policies of eighteenth- and nineteenth-century estates in the west and north-west of the county took other forms. Some were evidently aesthetic in character; others were simply the fads of agricultural improvers, such as the cherry plum (marabellum) hedges found on the carr-

stone of west Norfolk. Occasionally, hedges on the home farms of large estates include unusual mixes of species, perhaps for aesthetic reasons, perhaps because of the use of specimens passed on as superfluous to planting schemes in nearby parkland. On the Houghton estate, for example, the hedges in the area to the north of the park contain large quantities of sweet chestnut and beech. How far other species found in relatively recent hedges were deliberately placed there by landowners for aesthetic reasons is unclear, but rose was certainly planted with hawthorn in some enclosure hedges, as at Tottington in 1779 (NRO WLS LXI/II: see page 64).

Other regions

The boulder clay plateau, the north-east loams, Breckland and north-west Norfolk account for the overwhelming majority of the land area of Norfolk. But some smaller sub-regions, with their own distinctive character, also exist and should be briefly mentioned. One of the most important is the district of Gault clay on the edge of the Fens to the south of Downham Market. This area contains a complex and diverse range of soils, mainly clays of the Beccles and Burlingham associations but with restricted areas of sands and fen peat. It covers an area of around 100 square kilometres and carries a landscape which differs in a number of respects from that of the main mass of clay soils, formed in glacial drift, in the centre and south of the county. Settlement was more nucleated here, open fields more extensive and 'regular' in character, and much of the land, put down to pasture during the seventeenth century, remained under grass until relatively recently. This is the only part of the county in which the earthworks known as 'ridge and furrow', former open-field plough ridges, are still moderately common (Liddiard 1999). The district was also, to a greater extent than the main clay areas in the county, dominated by large landed estates, especially those based at Ryston, Stow Bardolph, and Stradsett.

Not surprisingly, the hedges found here have their own particular characteristics. They are relatively species-rich – an average of 4.3 species across all soil types, rising to 5 on the Beccles association soils. Hedges on 'irregular' boundaries, mainly roadsides, have an average of 4.4 species; those on piecemeal enclosure boundaries, 3.9; and those on straight boundaries, 3.8. This clustering of values at a relatively high level reflects both the soils, and the landscape history, of the district. Surviving estate maps (e.g., for Stradsett: NRO BC14/54; Wimbotsham, NRO Hare 6812, 1–2) show that in the mid seventeenth century much of the area still lay in arable open fields, although some parishes, such as Stow Bardolph, were already extensively enclosed. Most were enclosed piecemeal, as holdings were engrossed by large estates in the course of the later seventeenth and eighteenth centuries, with many boundaries subsequently being re-aligned and 'rationalised'. The overwhelming majority of hedges in the district, in other words, came into existence in the period between 1650 and 1850. The moist clay soils have allowed high rates of colonisation, a small number of ancient woods in the area providing a ready source of seeds and, perhaps, hedging plants. Yet the relative youth of the local boundary pattern has precluded the development of hedges of classic 'woodland relic' type: there are only two recorded examples of lime, hornbeam was noted in only 3 per cent of hedges, dog's mercury is rare, and only 9 per cent of recorded examples contain dogwood, in spite of the relatively damp character of most of the local soils.

Another distinctive district lies to the north of Norwich, in a rough triangle between Ringland and Easton in the south-west, Cawston in the north and Frettenham in the east. This is an area of acid glacio-fluvial sands, with poor, infertile soils, similar in general terms to those of Breckland. But the district covers a much smaller area, and is extensively dissected by river valleys. Like Breckland, much of the land remained as heath or open field until the enclosures of the late eighteenth and early nineteenth century; and as in Breckland, the average number of species found in the local hedges is surprisingly high, at 3.9 per thirty metres. In this respect, there is little difference between hedges of different ages: those of eighteenth- and nineteenth-century date, those created by earlier piecemeal enclosure, and those on 'irregular' boundaries, all have virtually the same average number of species (4.1, 4.5 and 3.8 respectively). But those on 'irregular' boundaries, especially on roadsides, are often characterised by large banks of hazel, blackthorn and maple, whereas those on late boundaries are dominated by hawthorn or blackthorn, with the usual suite of late colonisers and timber trees. Although in overall terms these soils are similar to those in Breckland, the hedgerow evidence perhaps suggests that there were rather more early hedges here. On these acid soils plants like hazel have often out-competed neighbours, thus bringing the average number of species present in thirty metre lengths down below that found in more recent hedges.

The reader may by now have tired of this rather extended discussion of the hedgerow characteristics of the various sub-regions of Norfolk. But mention must be made of the boundaries found in low-lying wetland areas. Narrow ribbons of damp peaty ground, which are characterised in particular by soils of the Isleham and Hanworth associations, occur widely on the floors of major valleys throughout Norfolk. Larger areas of drained wetland lie in the far west and east of the county: Fenland, and the Broads, respectively. In both of these districts, extensive areas of alluvium and silt lie towards the coast while deposits of peat occur inland. Most areas of peat soil, great and small, remained as open, undivided fen until planned enclosure in the post-medieval period, and today display highly rectilinear field patterns. But on silt soils boundaries are often much older. The Halvergate Marshes and adjacent areas, immediately to the west of Yarmouth, are characterised by a preponderance of curvilinear, serpentine ditches or dykes which were formed from the natural channels draining the salt marshes, as the area was 'inned' or embanked in the early medieval period: this was rich grazing marsh, exploited from isolated demesne farms (Williamson 1997, 62–71). On the other side of the county, in contrast, on the northern silt fens of Marshland to the west of Kings Lynn,

FIGURE 62.
View across the
Halvergate Marshes,
east Norfolk. Hedges
were unnecessary in
areas of marsh because
the dykes or ditches
served both to
demarcate property and
to confine livestock.

the land was studded with villages by the twelfth century and much of the land lay in arable open fields, the individual strips wider than those in the uplands and each separately ditched, or dyked. This pattern was preserved, in simplified form, by subsequent piecemeal enclosure and field amalgamation (Silvester 1988).

In all these watery lands hedges were never common because the dykes themselves provided good stock-proof barriers, and served to define separate properties (Figure 62). Nevertheless, hedges or hedge-like features are not entirely unknown. Where areas of peat ground are relatively confined, in the valleys of the smaller rivers, the ruler-straight drainage ditches are often accompanied by hedges. These are usually dominated by hawthorn but – compared with those of similar date on the adjacent 'uplands' – are relatively species-rich, often including examples of alder and willow. Where wetlands are extensive, in contrast, the situation is more variable. In the silt fens of Marshland scattered remains of hedges can be found in a number of places. Their date is

FIGURE 63.
Although true hedges are absent from the Broadland Marshes, many of the roads are bordered by lines of willows which, if managed in the traditional way – that is, pollarded at a height of 1.5 – 2 m – resemble an outgrown hedge. These examples flank a road in Halvergate parish, constructed in the 1830s.

uncertain: they occur on boundaries of medieval or early post-medieval origin, but may themselves be later additions. They are almost invariably in a poor condition, their management having evidently been neglected for a long period of time. Only a few continuous sections survive, few longer than thirty metres each, which are widely scattered across the district. It remains uncertain whether these represent survivors from a once much denser population. Hawthorn and blackthorn are the dominant plants, with small quantities of ash, rose, elder and privet. In normal circumstances this might suggest that the hedges are of no great antiquity, and this may indeed be the case. But it is also possible that, because they are growing at a distance from the 'uplands', on land reclaimed directly from salt marsh, it simply reflects an absence of proximate seed sources. However, one slightly richer hedge was noted during the survey, which included some examples of hazel; this was in the parish of Wiggenhall St Mary Magdalene and, perhaps significantly, was situated alongside an old road running close to the site of the medieval Priory of St. John.

The great tract of peat fens lying to the south of Marshland, enclosed in post-medieval times, is largely bare of hedges but there are a few exceptions, usually close to the margins of the adjacent 'uplands'. Here, on ruler-straight boundaries, hawthorn-dominated hedges sometimes accompany the drainage dykes, especially on roadsides. These also generally contain some blackthorn, elder and alder. In addition, close to the fen edge in Methwold and Wretton (and especially within the area known as Methwold Severals) there are a number of hedges composed of various mixtures of white, crack and sallow willow, together with some alder, alder buckthorn, hawthorn and blackthorn. Occasional examples of oak, maple, privet, elm and birch are also present.

Some are still maintained at a low height but most are now outgrown. These do not appear to be very old features of the landscape, and local tradition holds that they were established in the early or middle decades of the twentieth century, to provide shelter for crops. They seem to have originally been planted with willow alone. Most of the other species are adventitious, and the high number in many sample lengths (as many as 5 species per thirty metres) shows, once again, how hedges on moist and fertile soils can gain colonisers at a remarkably high rate.

On the eastern side of the county, the level drained marshlands of Halvergate and adjoining areas are completely devoid of true hedges. But lining many of the principal roads are lines of closely-planted willow trees which, when maintained in the traditional way, by pollarding at a height of around 1.5–2 m, make a line of continuous vegetation not dissimilar to an outgrown hedges (Figure 63). The trees seem to have been planted at intervals of around four metres, on the edge of the verge immediately above the flanking ditch. In some places – as on the branch road to Halvergate (around TG 438090–428069) – the trees are well preserved on both sides of the road. Elsewhere, as on the nearby 'Acle Straight' (the A47 to the west of Yarmouth), the remains are more patchy, many of the trees having been removed in comparatively recent times (the RAF aerial photographs of 1946 show that the lines were then much more continuous).

The willow rows appear to be very much a part of the 'traditional' Broadland scene, but they are in reality a fairly recent addition to the land-scape. It is true that early maps of the area do sometimes show lines of pollards; thus a map made in 1749 of an area of marsh to the west of Reedham church shows pollards growing beside some of the dykes (NRO MC 27/1, 501 X 4) while one surveyed in 1825 shows trees – again presumably willow pollards – growing on the side of a track running down to Oulton Dyke near Lowestoft, and also bordering some of the field dykes to the north (Barnes and Skipper 1995). But the vast majority of early maps do not show trees on the marshes, even though they might depict them in the hedgerows of the neighbouring upland, and the various nineteenth-century paintings of the marshes similarly attest the landscape's open, treeless quality. With few, if any, exceptions, the willow rows are associated with roads which were either newly created or extensively improved in the nineteenth century. Local tradition is unanimous regarding their purpose: the trees were planted to 'hold the shoulder of the road' – that is, to prevent the road from subsiding into the flanking ditches. The pollarding was essential to keep them low, so that they would not be brought down by the wind. It also allowed a narrow spacing, and thus a maximum amount of root structure to bind the ditch banks (Barnes and Skipper 1995, 200).

CHAPTER SIX

Conclusions

....

The origins and development of hedges

We can now summarise the principal findings of this study, and see how they qualify, or amplify, the earlier investigations of hedges briefly outlined in Chapter Two. All students of hedges owe a vast debt to the pioneering work of Hooper and Pollard, but in the light of subsequent research – including that presented here – it is clear that many of their basic conclusions, first advanced in the 1960s and 70s, require drastic modification. But our task, as we have already emphasised, is less to query the 'Hooper hypothesis' (or the 'Pollard postulate') than to explore how hedges really came into existence and changed over time – and why they display such variety in their composition, at both a local and a regional level.

Hooper suggested four ways in which a hedge could come into existence: through the management of strips of woodland vegetation around assarts ('woodland relic hedges'); by management of spontaneous shrub growth along the edge of fences, or on uncultivated banks and baulks; by planting a single species hedge; or by planting a multi-species hedge (Pollard *et al.* 1974, 86). We have failed to find any convincing evidence for Hooper's second proposed mode of origin, and none has appeared (so far as we know) in any other studies. The idea of the 'woodland relic hedge', however, does receive some support from the Norfolk evidence, although with important qualifications. Firstly, many of the key *herb* species identified as 'indicators' by Pollard in his initial study, especially dog's mercury, primrose, and bluebell, seem to have distributions which are related more to soil type than to hedgerow origins. Dog's mercury and primrose in particular have a close affinity with moist, neutral to calcareous soils, rather than an association with a particular kind of hedge. In 1974 Hooper and Pollard pointed to the close correlation between the distribution in Warwickshire of hedges containing dog's mercury, and that of woodland shown on seventeenth-century maps (Pollard *et al.* 1974, 103). They interpreted this as meaning that the hedges in question had been cut out of woodland, but our results would suggest that both distributions are in fact a consequence of soil type, both woodland and dog's mercury being a particular feature of heavy clay soils. Equally important is our observation that dog's mercury and primrose, while certainly associated with ancient woodland, will colonise beyond it quite rapidly, appearing even in some nineteenth-century hedges. Their relative abundance can certainly tell us something about the general history of the local landscape – the extent to which particular kinds of damp soil may have retained, or lost, their woodland cover over time. But the presence, or absence, of these plants can tell us little about the origins of individual hedges, and nothing at all about those hedges growing on soils too dry, acidic or infertile to sustain them. The importance of soils in determining the distribution of some of the key 'woodland relic' herbs has not, so far as we know, been demonstrated so clearly by previous research, although Addington noted in passing the absence of dog's mercury from the 'light and easily cultivated' soils in Tasburgh, and its concentration on the heavier soils (Addington 1978, 75). But other studies have anticipated our suggestion that, in well-wooded districts, dog's mercury in particular can spread for some distance along comparatively recent hedges (see, for example, Hussey 1987, 333).

Pollard suggested that, in addition to containing these distinctive herbs, hedges of 'woodland relic' type were particularly well mixed, and included an abundance of such slow-colonising shrubs as hazel, dogwood and maple, together with species like wild service which are rare outside ancient woodland. Hedges displaying these characteristics certainly occur, in some numbers, in Norfolk, and some other species – hornbeam and perhaps, in certain districts, elm – also appear to display 'woodland relic' characteristics. Moreover, the distribution of hedges containing lime, sessile oak or hornbeam seems to mirror, in broad terms, that of the ancient, semi-natural woodland in which these species are prominent. But there is considerable doubt about whether such hedges can have come into existence in the way originally envisaged by Pollard – that is, through management of the existing woodland understorey. Most occur on long linear features, such as roads or parish boundaries, rather than around small fields clearly assarted from the 'wastes'. A significant minority occur in hedges of piecemeal enclosure type which were, by definition, planted in places which had long been cleared of woodland, and cultivated as open-field arable. It is true, as we have seen, that hedges of 'woodland relic' character are amongst the oldest in any area and, where woodland is no longer a prominent feature in the landscape, they may indeed date back to early medieval times. But this is not *invariably* the case, to judge from the large minority occurring on piecemeal enclosure boundaries, which mainly came into existence in the fifteenth, sixteenth and seventeenth centuries.

This brings us to Hooper and Pollard's third and fourth categories of hedge – those planted with one, or with several, species. The vast majority of the county's hedges were deliberately planted, and mainly in the period after *c.* 1450. They resulted from the piecemeal enclosure of open fields; the planned, usually parliamentary enclosure of open field and commons; or the reorganisation of existing field patterns, especially by large landowners in the period after *c.* 1750. Hooper, as we have seen, believed that (except in some limited regions of England) the overwhelming majority of hedges had been planted with a single species, usually hawthorn. But Wendy Johnson's study in 1978 showed that there was abundant documentary evidence to the contrary, especially for the period before 1700 (Johnson 1978). The Norfolk evidence clearly supports Johnson's position. Not only do hedges of piecemeal enclosure type, as we have seen, sometimes display 'woodland relic' characteristics, suggesting that they must have been planted with material gathered from local woodland. They also differ very markedly in composition from the hawthorn-dominated hedges of eighteenth- and nineteenth-century date, in spite of the fact that they are in many case only slightly older: so markedly, in fact, that it is very hard to believe that they began life in the same way, as single-species hedges.

Wendy Johnson and others have argued that the eighteenth century saw a decisive shift from multi-species to single-species planting. While hedges planted solely with hawthorn and blackthorn had certainly existed in earlier centuries, the planting of mixed hedges was probably more usual. In part this may have been because hedges were viewed as useful sources of fuel, fodder and perhaps food, rather than just as stockproof barriers. Contemporaries were certainly aware of the fact that thorn hedges had fewer uses than mixed ones, providing no more than a stock-proof barrier. One, for example, castigated hedges of hawthorn on the grounds that 'its superfluous wood will not repay the labour of planting and cutting, nor is it productive of any profitable fruit' (Pitt 1813a, 54).

But multi-species planting was perhaps also encouraged by the difficulties of obtaining large quantities of hawthorn or blackthorn. In the course of the eighteenth century the proliferation of local commercial nurseries ensured that bulk quantities of hedging plants became more easily available. In part, this was a consequence of the fact that the advent of large-scale enclosure, especially by parliamentary act, stimulated the development of an appropriate supply network.

Norfolk was no exception to this development. William Aram set up his business at Lakenham near Norwich in 1760 and, joined from 1774 by his son-in-law John Mackie, supplied vast quantities of ornamental shrubs, forest trees and hedging plants to estates throughout the county (Williamson 1998a, 171; Harvey 1973, 15). A number of other commercial nurseries also sprang up in the county, or in the adjacent areas of Suffolk, including those established by George Lindley at Catton in 1796, and that run by Frederick Fitt at Hoveton in the 1770s, 80s and early 90s (Williamson 1998a, 171–2). Not surprisingly, as John Harvey has shown, there was a substantial fall in the price of hedging hawthorn between the mid eighteenth and the mid nineteenth century (Harvey 1973). Although some hedges continued to be planted with a mixture of species, especially hawthorn and blackthorn, the trend is clear enough, and it is in this light that we should interpret the repeated contrast made by some early nineteenth-century writers between 'new' hedges, of hawthorn, and 'old' ones, of mixed character (see pages 29–30). These men were observing not so much the variations resulting from age and the length of time different hedges had been available for colonisation, as relatively recent changes in the ways that hedges were actually planted. And it is in this context that we should note, once again, the problems encountered by researchers like Hall and Willmott in distinguishing, on the basis of species content alone, the antiquity of hedges planted at different times before the eighteenth century (Hall 1982, 105; Willmott 1980, 284). These changes in planting policy were in part a consequence of the greater availability of hedging plants like hawthorn and blackthorn, but they also reflected the fact that, in the eighteenth and nineteenth centuries, hedges were increasingly regarded solely as a means of providing a stock-proof barrier, rather than a source of fuel, fodder and the rest. This in turn reflected important social, tenurial and economic changes, such as the increasing importance of large landed estates and the decline of small owner-occupiers, and the availability of alternative sources of fuel (especially coal) and, perhaps, fodder (such as turnips).

Whatever individual hedges were first planted with, their flora developed thereafter in complex and diverse ways. As we have seen, there is no doubt that rates of colonisation varied, depending on soil type (damp and fertile soils supporting more species, and gaining them at a faster rate, than those growing in dry, leached environments) and proximity to seed source (in the form of ancient woods, or other hedges). These factors operated at both a regional level, and at a very local one, so that (for example) hedges growing on a small, unmapped area of sand within an extensive tract of boulder clay will be noticeably poorer in species, or one growing beside a small area of ancient woodland will be noticeably richer, than its neighbours. Previous studies, from Hooper onwards, have noted the importance of seed supply as a factor in colonisation rates, but the significance of soils has been consistently neglected. While one or two writers have speculated that soil characteristics might affect rates of colonisation (Hunter 1993, 114), the Norfolk evidence leaves no doubt that soil character is as important an influence on species diversity as age. A study embracing a wider geographical area would doubtless identify other important environmental influences, related in particular to climate. In upland districts, such as the Derbyshire Peak District or the uplands of southern Shropshire, colonisation rates are much slower than in the kind of area studied here (John Barnatt, pers comm.; Cameron and Pannet 1980a, 148).

Soil characteristics not only affect rates of colonisation. There is some evidence in the survey results that certain soil conditions encourage the displacement of some species by others. In such circumstances, as Richard Muir has emphasised, increasing age can serve to reduce, rather than to increase, the numbers of species in a hedge (Muir 1996, 60). While elm is the most obvious lateral coloniser, vigorously suckering along the length of a hedge, other species can also behave in this manner, most notably blackthorn and dogwood. The latter seems to out-compete its neighbours on damp sites in the claylands. Elm and blackthorn, in contrast, appear to invade most successfully on poor, leached soils, a pattern again mirrored elsewhere, especially on the London clays of south Hertfordshire and Middlesex, where many ancient hedges are overwhelmingly dominated by blackthorn; or on the coastal plains of Essex and the Suffolk Sandlings, where poor soils and proximity to the sea have ensured a clear preponderance of elm in older hedges (Figure 64). Plants producing an abundance of keys – ash, sycamore, maple – can also monopolise long lengths of hedge, perhaps especially (as we have suggested) where management was by coppicing rather than plashing. Management has certainly determined other aspects of hedge composition. As other writers and researchers have observed, plants may have been systematically removed from hedges during routine maintenance. Barberry is very rare in Norfolk hedges, perhaps because it has been destroyed by farmers with particular thoroughness in this paramount cereal-producing county. It has been known since at least the eighteenth century that it is a host for the fungus which produces black stem rust in wheat. Other species were added to existing hedges, either as timber or during 'gapping up' operations – the presence of the Duke of Argyll's Tea Plant in some west Norfolk hedges is the most obvious example of what must have been common practice. And in addition to the influence of soils, seed supply and management practices, the frequency of certain plants is also the consequence of particular patterns of natural development, with the presence of one species encouraging, or discouraging, the successful establishment of another. Elder is thus ubiquitous in hedges on the lighter soils, where abundant rabbit burrows provide plenty of areas of disturbed soil in which it can become established. On heavier land, in contrast, its presence is strongly correlated with that of elm. Elm occurs in 61 per cent of clayland hedges, elder in 53 per cent: elder occurs alone in only 19 per cent. This is presumably a recent development, resulting from the death of plants through Dutch elm disease and the opportunities thus provided for colonisation by elder.

Hedges thus have varied origins, and develop in varied ways depending on soils, seed supply, systems of management and other factors. Given this complexity, it is hardly surprising that there is no way of simply 'reading' the age, or origins, of a particular hedge from its present composition. Hedges of similar dates and origins planted in different districts can boast very different kinds, and numbers, of species. But even hedges planted at the same time on broadly similar soils, and in close proximity, can exhibit markedly different characteristics, resulting both from original differences in composition, and from variations in subsequent development associated with quite minor differences in environmental circumstances. We may imagine here three hedges planted during the early nineteenth century on clay soils – all based on real hedges, and on our observations of the processes of hedgerow development. One, established by a large landowner, was composed entirely of hawthorn with some oak standards, and lay towards the centre of what had formerly been a large common. A second was planted with hawthorn, and with standards of elm, when a rather smaller area of damp, low-lying clay common was enclosed. A third, planted by a small owner-occupier, was a mixture of hawthorn and blackthorn, with standards of sycamore and oak, and lay close to an area of woodland. All were subsequently managed in broadly the same way except the last, which in the early twentieth century was subject to a period of particularly rigorous coppicing.

FIGURE 64.
The harsh soils and coastal location of the Sandlings district of east Suffolk have ensured that most of the older hedges are largely composed of elm. Some may have been planted with this species, but in most cases other shrubs have probably been displaced by the species' habit of vigorous suckering.

Two hundred years later and the character of these three hedges has diverged even further. The first contains its original hawthorn and oak, together with some rose and ash; but the second now has hawthorn and elm in almost equal quantities, together with ash, blackthorn, rose, elder, and scattered specimens of dogwood, the seeds of which have been brought down by watercourses from older hedges on the adjacent areas of higher ground. The third now contains hawthorn, blackthorn, rose, oak, and great banks of sycamore and ash, monopolising the hedge for ten metres or more, as well as some maple and even the occasional hazel, colonising from the nearby woodland. One is still dominated by hawthorn, one is essentially a hawthorn/elm hedge, and one is mixed. But all these hedges were planted at the same time, on the same kind of soil.

Beyond the 'Hooper Hypothesis'

Because we generally have no way of knowing what a hedge was originally planted with, how it has been managed over the centuries, or how its surroundings have changed since it came into existence, it follows that we can say relatively little about the age or origins of any particular example from its current composition, except in terms so broad as to be virtually meaningless. A hedge first planted in the period after 1750 we could, in *most* circumstances, distinguish with confidence from one planted during the Middle Ages. But beyond this, we would be moving into much more uncertain and speculative terrain: and the reasons for this should by now be obvious. The 'Hooper Hypothesis', and any refinement of it – such as the formulation of local calibrations, taking account of soils and seed supply – could never work, except in the very broadest terms. Yet the sad thing is that, in stating this, we are merely repeating something which has been said by a wide variety of historians and ecologists since at least the mid 1970s. Indeed, it may well be that the idea that hedges can be 'dated', in a simple and direct way, by counting the number of species they contain will never be dislodged from the popular mind, like other myths about the English landscape – such as the notion that ancient sites, churches and the like align more often than chance would predict, having been intentionally placed on mysterious 'ley lines'. This again is an idea to which not a single professional archaeologist or landscape historian would give the slightest credence. Yet it remains firmly entrenched in popular culture and the media (Williamson and Bellamy 1983). Indeed, in an important sense the two concepts – hedge dating and ley lines – have much in common. Both allow the amateur to discover new things about the past in a relatively simple and direct way – looking at local hedges, or drawing lines on maps. And both, moreover, reinforce the not unhealthy concept that the past, even the quite remote past, is all around us, immanent in the landscape.

In saying all this our criticism is not so much of Hooper and his colleagues. They pioneered the scientific study of hedges, and it was in large measure because of their work that the idea of hedges as important *historical* features gained currency in England during the last third of the twentieth century. Moreover, as we have seen, in much of his published work Hooper argued a case much more complex than later 'hedge-daters' have generally allowed. Indeed, much of this short book has simply been a restatement of these original, more subtle arguments. If Hooper was 'guilty' of anything it was, perhaps, of not stating more publicly that his work, as it moved into the public domain, was being consistently over-simplified and misinterpreted.

Yet at the same time we would not want to suggest that there is nothing of historical importance that can be learnt from the study of hedges. Far from it: a knowledge of hedges, including a working knowledge of how to identify the principal hedgerow species, should form an essential element in the education of every landscape archaeologist or landscape historian. Radical differences in the composition of adjacent hedges, for example, are usually more historical than ecological in character, can suggest a *relative* chronology, and can indicate where significant reorganisations of the landscape – through, for example, planned enclosure – have taken place in the course of the post-medieval period. Such information is particularly useful when combined with an assessment of the shape of the boundaries in question – whether, for example, they display the sinuous, 'kinking' forms associated with piecemeal enclosure. But it is when we shift our focus from the individual hedge, or small groups of hedges, to the broad generality of hedges in a district or region that we can learn most. One way of looking at species diversity in hedges is simply as an index of the degree of continuity with the natural woodland of the area. Districts in which clearance was still at a relatively early stage when the first hedges were planted, even if few areas of managed woodland were subsequently retained, will generally have richer hedges than those in which woodland was removed more completely at an early date, and in which the first hedges were planted some time after this. In the former districts, such as the Norfolk claylands, even relatively young hedges can be comparatively diverse because existing hedges, and any surviving woodland, provided both a handy source of hedging plants and a ready reservoir of seeds. Where woodland cover has remained extensive up until this day, as in that part of Middlesex studied by Williams and Cunnington (1985), the differences in species content due to age may be quite limited. In areas in which discontinuity is greatest, in contrast – such as northwest Norfolk – it is the exceptions to the general pattern which are of especial interest: where, rarely, ancient hedges with 'woodland relic' characteristics occur, for these indicate that some woodland must have survived in the vicinity up until the time that the hedges in question were planted, and also – in most cases – that these hedges are therefore very old. Yet even in old enclosed areas like the Norfolk claylands hedges which are thoroughly mixed in character, and which contain particularly large quantities of woodland species, may provide the historian with some indication of which are likely to be the oldest boundaries in the landscape (see page 98).

But relatively recent hedges also have their stories to tell. Together with an analysis of field shapes, an examination of species content reveals very clearly the extent to which landowners reorganised the field patterns in long-enclosed areas in the course of the eighteenth and nineteenth centuries, by straightening boundaries, removing pollards and replacing mixed with single-species hedges. In some areas of 'ancient countryside' the majority of field boundaries, away from public roads, are no older than those in the 'planned countryside' districts of parliamentary enclosure. This obsession with 'tidying up' these ancient landscapes on the part of the larger landowners is one manifestation of a wider fashionable interest in 'improvement' which determined not only that all areas of common land and open field should be systematically removed, but that the fields that replaced them should be hedged in an appropriately 'modern' way – with hedges which provided no regular benefits for farmers in terms of fuel or fodder. The new, uniform modes of planting – like the contemporaneous shift away from pollarding – reflected both the aesthetic preferences, and the economic requirements, of the class who now controlled the land. Changes in the character of hedges, in other words, are in part related to the decline of a peasant economy and the increasing consolidation of ownership in the hands of large landowners. And as we have seen, the spirit of aristocratic 'improvement' created entirely new types of hedge, even more divorced from those of local tradition: most notably, the Scots pine 'rows' which are such a feature of Breckland.

These developments and tendencies – the relationship between land ownership, rural economy and choice of hedging plant – can again be paralleled throughout the country: at one extreme, in the relatively recent but multi-species hedges established by smallholders in Shropshire, for example (Cameron and Pannett 1980b); and at the other, in the overwhelming dominance of hawthorn in parliamentary enclosure hedges throughout much of lowland England, and in the use by large nineteenth-century estates of such exotic plants as tamarisk (*Tamarix gallica*), which can be found sporadically in hedges along the south coast westwards from Hampshire to Cornwall.

Hedges and landscape character

Although much of the variation in the character of hedges, in Norfolk as elsewhere, is a consequence of historical factors, some as we have seen is the direct consequence of purely natural influences, and especially of soil character. Privet, for example, is a frequent feature of the hedges growing on the light calcareous soils of west Norfolk but is relatively rare on the clays of the southeast; holly, in contrast, is mainly associated with the more acidic clays and loams, while dogwood is largely restricted to the moister soils. But, as will by now have become apparent, the natural environment also had a number of indirect influences on hedgerow character, influencing the extent of early clearance, the character of medieval and post-medieval farming, and structures of land ownership – and thus the type and chronology of enclosure. Of course, soils were not the only factor to influence the character of boundaries: but these, together with other aspects of the 'cultural landscape', such as the forms of settlement, are nevertheless strongly correlated with soil types (Williamson 2003, 22–3).

Archaeologists, those working in the public service especially – in County Council archaeological departments, or in English Heritage – have recently become very interested in mapping the character of regional landscapes, an interest fuelled in part by the new computer mapping technology of Geographical Information Systems, in part by recent government interest in preserving and enhancing a 'sense of place' among the community at large, and in part by a growing awareness of the historical importance of the everyday landscape, and the need to ensure that new developments do not impact negatively upon it. 'Historic Landscape Characterisation' ('HLC') projects have recently been completed, or are currently underway, in many counties, including Norfolk (Aldred 2002; Aldred and Fairclough 2003; Countryside Commission 1996; Fairclough 1994, 2002, 1999; Fairclough, Lambrick and Hopkins 2002; Rippon 2004, 53–5; Clark, Darlington and Fairclough 2004). These essentially involve the meticulous mapping of field and road patterns, as shown on modern OS maps, and their classification in terms of morphological characteristics and supposed historical origins – much as in

FIGURE 65.
The landscape of
north-west Norfolk
near Houghton: large
fields, mainly bounded
by straight species-poor
hedges which contain
few trees, and blocks of
estate woodland.

FIGURE 66.
The landscape of
north-east Norfolk has
suffered badly from
intensive modern
farming, but Sloley is
one place where it is
still possible to savour
the traditional land-
scape of the region.
The hedges – partly
created by piecemeal
enclosure, partly by
eighteenth- and nine-
teenth-century
reorganisation and the
enclosure of common
land – are moderately
species-rich and thickly
studded with oak trees.

our Figure 25, but with greater detail and precision. Not all landscape archae-ologists are equally enthusiastic about this procedure, about how it has been carried out, or how it has been applied to the wider field of planning and public policy. No standardised methodology has yet been developed, so the results from adjacent counties often cannot be easily compared. Many of these projects have been undertaken by individuals more familiar with the use of GIS to examine archaeological distributions than with the complex history of the rural landscape. The very term 'landscape characterisation' is really a misnomer – it is a procedure which characterises field shapes, not all the other elements which make up a landscape. Above all, the landscape is characterised in *plan*, as if viewed from above, whereas in reality people usually experience it on the ground. This is peculiar, given that a generation of archaeologists, especially prehistorians, have emphasised that we should think of past sites and

FIGURE 67.
View in south Norfolk:
a winding lane, flanked
by mixed hedges, rich
with elm, ash,
dogwood and maple.

landscapes as they were experienced by contemporaries, as three-dimensional arrangements of spaces and structures, not as we prefer to record them, in two-dimensional plans (e.g. Barrett 1994).

It is these last two problems which have a particular relevance here. The character of hedges – the species of which they are composed, the ways in which they are managed, whether or not they are accompanied by banks or ditches and what form these take, how many and what kinds of trees they contain – it is these things, more than the shapes of the fields they bound, which really define the character of a region's landscape. These matters are largely if not entirely ignored in the majority of 'characterisation' projects. Most would classify both Breckland and north-west Norfolk simply as areas of late, rectilinear, planned enclosure. Yet because a large proportion of the field boundaries in the former region are defined by lines of Scots pines, while those in the latter are hawthorn hedges, the whole 'feel' of the two landscapes is radically different. Moreover, even in north-west Norfolk the essence of the landscape would not be fully captured by simply classifying it as a 'late rectilinear field pattern', not least because the roads from which the landscape is primarily experienced are often very serpentine. Its character derives as much from the structure and appearance of the boundaries which define the fields: low, species-poor hawthorn hedges, generally rather sparsely timbered. In a similar way, the landscape of north-east Norfolk owes more to the dominance of oak standards in moderately species-rich hedges, raised in many cases on low banks, than it does to the shape of the fields that these surround; while the landscape of the southern claylands is, above all, characterised by the great mixed hedges which line the principal roads, with their great banks of hazel, maple and dogwood, so colourful in the autumn, their abundance of ash and elm, and their ancient oaks (Figures 65, 66, and 67). In other words, by concentrating on the shape of fields alone, and ignoring the character of boundaries, historic landscape characterisation fails singly to capture the essence of local distinctiveness.

This is particularly important when we come to consider the practical contribution to landscape conservation that characterisation exercises might make. For while there are relatively few areas in which new field patterns will be created in the future – patterns which might need to be modelled on the existing structures of the landscape – there are many existing boundaries from which hedges were removed in the late twentieth century, which may well become hedged again in the near future. For the trend towards hedge removal which, as we have seen, continued unabated through the 1950s, 60s and 70s, and began to ease in the 1980s, is now being reversed. In Norfolk, as elsewhere, this is in part a consequence of wider changes in social attitudes. Post-War worries about food shortages have been replaced by widespread concerns about the degradation of the natural environment. Encouraged by the activities of the Farming and Wildlife Advisory Groups and (in the case of Norfolk) the County Council, many farmers and landowners began to replant hedges during the 1980s. Spurred on, in addition, by an active interest in game conservation and worries about the decline of birds like the grey partridge, the rate of replanting increased markedly during the 1990s and, although the grubbing-out of hedgerows still continued in places, gains and losses began to move into equilibrium. Various government schemes intended to redirect resources away from over-production towards nature conservation – especially Countryside Stewardship – provided financial incentives. As a result, rows of grow-tubes are as familiar a sight in the countryside of today as the mangled wreckage of bulldozed hedges was in that of the 1960s.

This is a welcome development. But when we examine what lurks within the tubes it is hard to avoid a sense of disappointment (Figure 68). In most cases, little or no attention has been paid to issues of local landscape character, to the kinds of species found in surviving hedges in the vicinity. A standard mix of shrubs commonly found in 'ancient' hedges – dogwood, maple, hazel, spindle and the rest – is everywhere employed, even in areas of relatively recent enclosure. More worryingly, species rare or alien to particular localities appear with monotonous regularity: guelder rose, for example, is frequently included in these ersatz ancient hedges, although it is a relatively uncommon hedgerow plant in Norfolk, even in old hedges on the southern claylands (Figure 69). If landscape character matters, then more attention should be paid to the form and composition of our hedges, and to perpetuating this when hedges are re-established. We hope that this short volume will have increased awareness of this issue, not only in Norfolk, but also more widely.

In one respect these new hedges encapsulate just another phase in the long and complex history of our rural landscape. They reflect new attitudes, emerging in the late twentieth century, about the purpose and function of the countryside. For today the majority of hedges, especially in an intensively arable county like Norfolk, are quite irrelevant to the needs of modern agriculture. We plant them to enhance the appearance of the countryside, and for their value to wildlife. These hedges, with their improbable and often inappropriate combinations of species, are as much an artefact of our escapist and heritage-conscious times as the no-nonsense, single-species, ruler-straight hedges were of the more practical world of the eighteenth or nineteenth centuries, which were themselves so different from the diverse plantings made by earlier generations of farmers, keen to maximise their supply of firewood and, perhaps, fruit and fodder.

The planting of these new mixed hedges has another important consequence. Although, at the present time, most can still be recognised for the fakes they are – either by the remains of mulch mats or grow-tubes, or through the repetitive and regular spacing of the constituent species – this will not be true for long. As the tell-tale traces of recent planting disappear, and as some plants flourish and spread while others fail and die, they will soon more closely resemble their models. The early twenty-first century is, perhaps, the last time that a study such as the one we have described here could be undertaken, with any serious hope of unravelling the complex history of our hedgerows.

FIGURE 68.
One of many hedges
planted in Norfolk over
the last two decades,
reversing the tide of
destruction which
swept the county in the
1960s and 70s.

FIGURE 69.
Guelder rose, widely
planted in modern
'mixed' hedges in
Norfolk, is in reality a
fairly rare plant in the
county.

Bibliography

Addington, S. (1978) 'The hedgerows of Tasburgh', *Norfolk Archaeology* 37, 70–83.

Aldred, O. (2002) 'Somerset and Exmoor National Park Historic Landscape Characterisation Project', *Society for Landscape Studies Newsletter*, Winter 2002, 3–5.

Aldred, O. and Fairclough, G. (2003) *Historic Landscape Characterisation: Taking Stock of the Method*, London.

Allison, K. J. (1957) 'The sheep-corn husbandry of Norfolk in the sixteenth and seventeenth centuries', *Agricultural History Review* 5, 12–30.

Bacon, R. N. (1844) *The Report on the Agriculture of Norfolk*, Norwich.

Bailey, M. (1989) *A Marginal Economy? East Anglian Breckland in the Later Middle Ages*, Cambridge.

Bailey, M. (1990) 'Sand into gold: the evolution of the foldcourse system in west Suffolk, 1200–1600', *Agricultural History Review* 38, 40–57.

Baird, W. and Tarrant, J. (1970) *Hedgerow Destruction in Norfolk, 1946–1970*, Norwich.

Barnes, G. (2003) *Woodland in Norfolk: A Landscape History*, unpublished PhD, School of History, University of East Anglia.

Barnes, G. and Skipper, K. (1995) 'Pollarded willows in the Norfolk Broads', *Quarterly Journal of Forestry* 89, 3, 196–200.

Barnes, G., Parmenter, J. and Williamson, T. (1998) 'The Norfolk Hedge and Boundary Survey: an interim report', *Transactions of the Norfolk and Norwich Naturalists Society* 31, 384–99.

Barrett, J. (1994) *Fragments from Antiquity: An Archaeology of Social Life in Britain, 2900–1200 BC*, Oxford.

Beckett, G., Bull, A. and Stevenson, R. (1999) *The Flora of Norfolk*, King's Lynn.

Blatchley, J. ed. (1982) *D. E. Davy: A Journal of Excursions through the County of Suffolk 1823–1844*, Suffolk Records Society Vol. 24, Woodbridge.

Boys, J. (1813) *General View of the Agriculture of Kent*, London.

Brooks, A. (1975) *Hedging: A Practical Conservation Handbook*, London.

Brown, A. F. J. (1996) *Prosperity and Poverty: Rural Essex, 1700–1815*, Chelmsford.

Burleigh, G. and Sawford, B. (1979) 'Hertfordshire hedges: Clothall', *Hertfordshire Past and Present*, 18–19.

Caird, J. (1852) *English Agriculture 1851–2*, London.

Cameron, R. A. D. (1984) 'The biology and history of hedges: exploring the connections', *Biologist* 31, 4, 203–9.

Cameron, R. A. D. and Pannett, D. J. (1980a) 'Hedgerow shrubs and landscape history in the West Midlands', *Arboricultural Journal* 4, 147–52.

Cameron, R. A. D. and Pannett, D. J. (1980b) 'Hedgerow shrubs and landscape history: some Shropshire examples', *Field Studies* 5, 177–94.

Campbell, B. (1981) 'The extent and layout of commonfields in eastern Norfolk', *Norfolk Archaeology* 28, 5–33.

Chapman, J. (1987) 'The extent and nature of parliamentary enclosure', *Agricultural History Review* **35**, 25–35.

Chatwin, C. P. (1961) *East Anglia and Adjoining Areas*, London.

Clark, J., Darlington, J. and Fairclough, G. (2004) *Using Historic Landscape Characterisation*, London.

Clarke, W. G. (1908) 'Some Breckland characteristics', *Transactions of the Norfolk and Norwich Naturalists Society* **8**, 555–78.

Clarke, W. G. (1925) *In Breckland Wilds*, London.

Cook, M. (1676) *The Manner of Raising, Ordering and Improving Forest Trees*, London.

Council for the Protection of Rural England (1973) *Hedges*, London.

Countryside Commission (1996) *Views from the Past: Historic Landscape Character in the English Countryside*, Cheltenham.

Dannatt, N. (1996) 'Thetford Forest: its history and development', in *Thetford Forest Park: the ecology of a pine forest*, eds P. Ratcliffe and J. Claridge, Forestry Commission Technical Paper **13**, Edinburgh.

Davenport, F. G. (1967) *The Economic Development of a Norfolk Manor, 1086–1565*, London.

Davison, A. (1973) 'The agrarian history of Hargham and Snetterton as recorded in the Buxton Mss', *Norfolk Archaeology* **35**, 335–55.

Davison, A. (1990) *The Evolution of Settlement in Three Parishes in South East Norfolk*, published as *East Anglian Archaeology* **49**.

Dowdeswell, W. H. (1987) *Hedgerows and Verges*, London.

Dulley, F. (1979) 'Hertfordshire hedges: Aldenham', *Hertfordshire Past and Present*, 16–17.

Evans, J. and O'Connor, T. (1999) *Environmental Archaeology: Principles and Methods*, Stroud.

Everitt, A. (1977) 'River and wold: reflections on the historical origins of regions and *pays*', *Journal of Historical Geography* **3**, 1–19.

Eyre, S. R. (1955) 'The curving ploughland strip and its historical implications', *Agricultural History Review* **3**, 80–94.

Fairclough, G. (1994) '"Landscapes from the past – only human nature". English Heritage's approach to historic landscapes', *Landscape Issues* **11**, 64–72.

Fairclough, G. (2002) *Historic Landscape Characterisation: Template Project Design for EH-Supported Country-Wide HLC projects*, London.

Fairclough, G. ed. (1999) *Historic Landscape Characterisation: Papers Presented at an English Heritage Seminar, December 1998*, London.

Fairclough, G., Lambrick, G. and Hopkins, D. (2002) 'Historic landscape characterisation and a Hampshire case study', in *Europe's Cultural Landscape: Archaeologists and the Management of Change*, eds G. Fairclough and S. Rippon, Brussels, 69–83.

Fitzherbert, J. (1534) *Five Hundred Pointes of Good Husbandrie*, London.

Fowler, P. J. (1974) 'Hedged about with doubt', *Bristol Archaeological Research Group Bulletin* **5** (2), 25–9.

Funnell, B. (1993) 'Solid geology', in *An Historical Atlas of Norfolk*, ed. P. Wade-Martins, Norwich, 12–13.

Gairdner, J. ed. (1896) *The Paston Letters, 1422–1509*, Westminster.

Gilpin, W. (1809) *Observations On Several Parts of the Counties of Cambridge, Norfolk, Suffolk and Essex. Also On Several Parts of North Wales; Relative Chiefly to Picturesque Beauty, in Two Tours, the Former Made in the Year 1769. The Latter in the Year 1773*, London.

Hall, J. (1982) 'Hedgerows in West Yorkshire: the Hooper method examined', *Yorkshire Archaeological Journal* **54**, 103–9.

Halstead, P. (1996) 'Ask the fellows who lop the hay: leaf fodder in the mountains of north-west Greece', *Rural History: Economy, Society, Culture* **9**, 211–35.

Bibliography

Hammond, B. and J. L. (1911) *The Village Labourer 1760–1832*, London.

Harvey, J. (1973) 'Forest trees and their prices before 1850', *Quarterly Journal of Forestry* **58**, 8.

Havinden, M. (1961) 'Agricultural progress in open-field Oxfordshire', *Agricultural History Review* **9**, 73–83.

Helliwell, D. R. (1975) 'The distribution of woodland plant species in some Shropshire hedgerows', *Journal of Biological Conservation* **7**, 61–72.

Hewlett, G. (1974) 'Reconstructing a historical landscape from field and documentary evidence: Otford in Kent', *Agricultural History Review* **21**, 94–110.

Hoare, C. M. (1918) *The History of an East Anglian Soke*, Bedford.

Hodge, C., Burton, R., Corbett, W., Evans, R. and Scale, R. (1984) *Soils and their Use in Eastern England*, Harpenden.

Holderness, B. A. (1985) 'East Anglia and the Fens', in *The Agrarian History of England and Wales*, Volume V, 2, ed. J. Thirsk, Cambridge, 119–245.

Holland, H. (1813) *General View of the Agriculture of Cheshire*, London.

Hooper, M. D. (1970) 'Dating hedges', *Area* **4**, 63–5.

Hooper, M. D. (1971) 'Hedges in local history', in *Hedges and Local History*, National Council of Social Services, London.

Hoskins, W. G. (1967) *Fieldwork in Local History*, London.

Hunter, J. (1993) 'The age of hedgerows on a Bocking estate', *Essex Archaeology and History* **24**, 114–17.

Hunter, J. (1997) 'The age of Cressing field boundaries', *Essex Archaeology and History* **28**, 151–5.

Hussey, T. (1987) 'Hedgerow history', *Local Historian*, 327–42.

Johnson, C. J. (1980) 'The statistical limitations of hedge dating', *Local Historian* **14**, 28–33.

Johnson, W. (1978) 'Hedges: a review of some early literature', *Local Historian* **13**, 195–204.

Johnson, W. (1981) 'The application of hedge-dating techniques in south Norfolk', *Norfolk Archaeology* **28**, 182–91.

Kent, N. (1796) *General View of the Agriculture of Norfolk*, London.

Kerridge, E. (1967) *The Agricultural Revolution*, London.

Lambert, S. ed. (1977) *House of Commons Sessional Papers of the Eighteenth Century: George III; Reports of the Commissioners of Land Revenue, 8–11, 1792*, Delaware.

Land Use Consultants 1999. *National Research on Locally Distinctive Hedgerows: Final Report*, London.

Liddiard, R. (1999) 'The distribution of ridge and furrow in Norfolk: ploughing practice and subsequent land use', *Agricultural History Review* **47**, 1–6.

Marshall, W. (1787) *The Rural Economy of Norfolk*, 2 volumes, London.

Marshall, W. (1796) *Planting and Rural Ornament*, London.

Middleton, J. (1813) *General View of the Agriculture of the County of Middlesex*, London.

Mingay, G. E. (1997) *Parliamentary Enclosure in England: An Introduction to its Causes, Incidence and Impact*, London.

Moreton, C. and Rutledge, P. eds (1996) *Skayman's Book: Farming and Gardening in Late Medieval Norfolk*, Norfolk Record Society **LXI**, Norwich.

Muir, R. (1995) 'Hedgerow ecology and the landscape historian', *Naturalist* **120**, 115–18.

Muir, R. (1996) 'Hedgerow dating: a critique', *Naturalist* **121**, 59–64.

Murphy, P. (1993) 'Early farming in Norfolk' in An Historical Atlas of Norfolk, ed. P. Wade-Martins, Norfolk Museums Service.

Muir, R. and Muir, N. (1997) *Hedgerows: Their History and Wildlife*, London.

Nau, B. S. and Rands, E. B. (1975) 'A comparative study of hedges on the boulder clay and lower greensand in the Maulden Area, *Bedfordshire Naturalist* **30**, 39–52.

Norden, J. (1607) *The Surveyor's Dialogue*, London.

Peglar, S. M., Fritz, S. C. and Birks, H. J. B. (1989) 'Vegetation and land use history at Diss, Norfolk', *Journal of Ecology* 77, 203–22.

Perry, P. J. (1974) *British Farming in the Great Depression*, London.

Pitchforth, H. (2001) *A Hidden Countryside: Discovering Ancient Tracks, Fields and Hedges*, Witham.

Pitt, W. (1813a) *General View of the Agriculture of the County of Northampton*, London.

Pitt, W. (1813b) *General View of the Agriculture of the County of Stafford*, London.

Pollard, E. (1973) 'Hedges, VII. Woodland relic hedges in Huntingdonshire and Peterborough, *Journal of Ecology* **61**, 343–52.

Pollard, E., Hooper, M. D. and Moore, N. W. (1974) *Hedges*, Collins New Naturalist Series, London.

Postgate, M. R. (1973) 'Field systems of East Anglia', in *Studies of Field Systems in the British Isles*, eds R. A. Butler and A. R. H. Baker, Cambridge, 281–324.

Priest, Rev. St John (1813) *General View of the Agriculture of the County of Buckinghamshire*, London.

Rackham, O. (1976) *Trees and Woodlands in the British Landscape*, London.

Rackham, O. (1986) *The History of the Countryside*, London.

Reed, M. (1979) *The Buckinghamshire Landscape*, London.

Reed, M. (1981) 'Pre-parliamentary enclosure in the East Midlands, 1550 to 1750, and its impact on the landscape', *Landscape History* **3**, 60–8.

Richens, R. H. (1983) *Elm*, Cambridge.

Rippon, S. (2004) *Historic Landscape Analysis*, London.

Roberts, B. and Wrathmell, S. (2002) *Region and Place*, London.

Roden, D. (1973) 'The field systems of the Chiltern Hills and their environs', in *Studies of Field Systems in the British Isles*, eds R. A. Butler and A. R. H. Baker, Cambridge, 325–74.

Rodwell, W. R. and Rodwell, K. (1993) *Rivenhall: Investigations of a Roman Villa, Church and Village*, Chelmsford Archaeological Trust Report **42**, Chelmsford.

Rogers, E. V. (1984) 'Sessile oak – *Quercus petraea* Leibe in Norfolk', *Transactions of the Norfolk and Norwich Naturalists Society* **17**, 291–7.

Rogerson, A. (1995) *Fransham: An Archaeological and Historical Study of a Parish on the Norfolk Boulder Clay*, unpublished PhD Thesis, Centre of East Anglian Studies, University of East Anglia.

Saunders, H. W. (1917) 'Estate management at Raynham 1661–86 and 1706', *Norfolk Archaeology* **19**, 39–67.

Short, D. (1979) 'Hertfordshire hedges: Ashwell', *Hertfordshire Past and Present*, 22–3.

Silvester, R. (1988) *Marshland and the Nar Valley, Norfolk*, published as *East Anglian Archaeology* **45**, Dereham.

Skipper, K. (1989) *Wood-Pasture: the Landscape of the Norfolk Claylands in the Early Modern Period*, unpublished MA thesis, Centre of East Anglian Studies, University of East Anglia.

Slotte, H. (2001) 'Harvesting of leaf-hay shaped the Swedish landscape', *Landscape Ecology* **16**, 691–702.

Smith, A. Hassell (1974) *County and Court: Government and Politics in Norfolk 1558–1603*, Oxford.

Spray, M. (1981) 'Holly as fodder in England', *Agricultural History Review* **29**, 97–110.

Stevenson, W. (1815a) *General View of the Agriculture of Dorset*, London.

Stevenson, W. (1815b) *General View of the Agriculture of Lancashire*, London.

Streeter, D. and Richardson, R. (1982) *Discovering Hedgerows*, London.

Sussams, K. (1996) *The Breckland Archaeological Survey*, Ipswich.

Bibliography

Taylor, C. (1973) *The Cambridgeshire Landscape*, London.

Theobald, J. (2000) *Changing Landscapes, Changing Economies: Holdings in Woodland High Suffolk 1600–1850*, unpublished PhD Thesis, University of East Anglia.

Thirsk, J. (1987) *England's Agricultural Regions and Agrarian History 1500–1750*, London.

Tillyard, R. (1976) 'Hedge dating in north Norfolk: the Hooper Method examined', *Norfolk Archaeology* **36**, 272–9.

Turner, M. (1980) *English Parliamentary Enclosure*, Folkestone.

Turner, M. (1982) 'The landscape of parliamentary enclosure', in *Discovering Past Landscapes*, ed. M. Reed, London, 132–66.

Turner, S. (2004) 'The changing ancient landscape: south-west England c. 1700–1900', *Landscapes* **5** (**1**), 18–34.

Wade-Martins, P. (1980) *Village Sites in the Launditch Hundred*, published as *East Anglian Archaeology* **10**, East Dereham.

Wade Martins, S. and Williamson, T. (1996) *The Farming Journal of Randall Burroughes 1794–1799*, Norfolk Record Society, Norwich.

Wade Martins, S. and Williamson, T. (1999) *Roots of Change: Farming and the Landscape in East Anglia 1700–1870*, Exeter.

Williams, L. R. and Cunnington, W. (1985) 'Dating a hedgerow landscape in Middlesex: Fryent Country Park', *London Naturalist* **64**, 7–22.

Williamson, T. (1993) *The Origins of Norfolk*, Manchester.

Williamson, T. (1997) *The Norfolk Broads: A Landscape History*, Manchester.

Williamson, T. (1998a) *The Archaeology of the Landscape Park: Garden Design in Norfolk, England, c. 1680–1840*, British Archaeological Reports British Series **268**, Oxford.

Williamson, T. (1998b) 'The "Scole-Dickleburgh Field System" revisited', *Landscape History* **20**, 19–28.

Williamson, T. (2000) 'Understanding enclosure', *Landscapes* **1** (**1**), 56–79.

Williamson, T. (2002) *The Transformation of Rural England: Farming and the Landscape 1700–1870*, Exeter.

Williamson, T. (2003) *Shaping Medieval Landscapes: Settlement, Society, Environment*, Macclesfield.

Williamson, T. and Bellamy, L. (1983) *Ley Lines in Question*, London.

Willmott, A. (1980) 'The woody species of hedge with special reference to age in Church Broughton Parish, Derbyshire', *Journal of Ecology* **68**, 269–286.

Wilson, R. (1979) *The Hedgerow Book*, David and Charles, Newton Abbot.

Witney, K. P. (1990) 'The woodland economy of Kent, 1066–1348', *Agricultural History Review* **38**, 20–39.

Yelling, J. A. (1977) *Common Field and Enclosure in England 1450–1850*, London.

Young, A. (1804) *General View of the Agriculture of Norfolk*, London.

Young, A. (1813) *General View of the Agriculture of Hertfordshire*, London.